The Essential
KEN WILBER

The Essential
KEN WILBER

An Introductory Reader

SHAMBHALA
Boston & London
1998

SHAMBHALA PUBLICATIONS, INC.
Horticultural Hall
300 Massachusetts Avenue
Boston, Massachusetts 02115
www.shambhala.com

12 11 10 9 8 7 6

Printed in the United States of America

☉ This edition is printed on acid-free paper that meets the
American National Standards Institute Z39.48 Standard.
Distributed in the United States by Random House, Inc.,
and in Canada by Random House of Canada Ltd

Library of Congress Cataloging-in-Publication Data
Wilber, Ken.
    The essential Ken Wilber: an introductory reader.—1st ed.
      p. cm.
    Includes bibliographical references.
    ISBN 1-57062-379-1 (pbk.: alk. paper)
      1. Consciousness. 2. Subconsciousness. 3. Self-perception.
    4. Psychology—Philosophy. 5. East and West. I. Title.
    BF311.W579 1998   98-4444
    191—dc21   CIP

Contents

About This Book   vii

The Divine Play   1
The Message of the Mystics   3
What Is Meditation?   5
The Perennial Philosophy   7
The Transpersonal   9
The Nondual Vision   12
Of Physicists and Mystics   16
The Real Self   21
"I-I"   27
Egolessness   31
The Witness Exercise   36
Levels of Consciousness   41
Constant Consciousness   44
The Great Chain of Being   49
Holons and Hierarchy   55
Reality Is Made of Holons   61
The Spectrum of Consciousness   65
The Centaur   73
Healing the Bodymind Split   75

Experiential, Intellectual, and Spiritual   85

The Pre/Trans Fallacy   88

Rationality Means Perspective   92

The Romantic View   95

The Big Three: I, We, and It   101

The Integral Approach   102

Integral Practice   105

Completing the Great Chain   108

Waves and Streams in Consciousness   115

Buddhism and the Stages of Development   123

One Hand Clapping   128

You Are Already Aware   131

One Taste   135

Translation versus Transformation   140

Contemplating Art   144

Was Carl Jung a Mystic?   147

The Real Archetypes   150

Academic Religion   152

The Value of Polemics   153

Sleep, Dreams, and Dreamless Sleep   156

The Meaning of Illness   162

The Moment of Death   170

The Ultimate Spiritual Test   172

Spiritual Unfolding   176

An Ounce of Laughter   185

Just This   186

Books by Ken Wilber: An Annotated List   187

Index   193

About This Book

Ken Wilber has been praised as one of the greatest thinkers of our time. His full-spectrum model of the stages of human growth and development, from birth to enlightenment, have made him a leading theorist in the study of human consciousness. Over the course of sixteen books, he has developed this theoretical system embracing the essential truths of East and West, uniting ancient wisdom with modern science. It is the foundation for an integral method of examining virtually any other field of study or endeavor: evolutionary theory, physics, anthropology, sociology, psychoanalysis, religion, art, literature, and so on. But despite Wilber's skill in explaining complex philosophical ideas, much of his work is written for a professional or academic audience and remains beyond the reach of more casual readers. In this book, I have therefore excerpted short, accessible passages from his writings so that people who have not read his more technical works might gain some appreciation for this important and sometimes controversial thinker.

This collection is not meant as a crash course in Ken Wilber; a complete and coherent picture of his thought would be impossible to attain by reading short excerpts, since he has patiently developed his ideas over the course of several books. However, there are many passages that can be enjoyed in themselves for informative, stimulating, or inspirational reading.

As an appreciative reader who became acquainted with these writings in the course of my work as an editor for Shambhala Publications, I selected nontechnical passages that impart the essence and flavor of Wilber's writings and that touch on his major concerns. I hope the selections will encourage readers to explore his ideas in greater depth. An annotated list of his works at the back of this book is added as a guide for further reading.

KENDRA CROSSEN BURROUGHS

The Divine Play

As Plotinus knew: Let the world be quiet. Let the heavens and the earth and the seas be still. Let the world be waiting. Let the self-contraction relax into the empty ground of its own awareness, and let it there quietly die. See how Spirit pours through each and every opening in the turmoil, and bestows new splendor on the setting Sun and its glorious Earth and all its radiant inhabitants. See the Kosmos dance in Emptiness; see the play of light in all creatures great and small; see finite worlds sing and rejoice in the play of the very Divine, floating on a Glory that renders each transparent, flooded by a joy that refuses time or terror, that undoes the madness of the loveless self and buries it in splendor.

Indeed, indeed: let the self-contraction relax into the empty ground of its own awareness, and let it there quietly die. See the Kosmos arise in its place, dancing madly and divine, self-luminous and self-liberating, intoxicated by a Light that never dawns nor ceases. See the worlds arise and fall, never caught in time or turmoil, transparent images shimmering in the radiant Abyss. Watch the mountain walk on water, drink the Pacific in a single gulp, blink and a billion universes rise and fall, breathe out and create a Kosmos, breathe in and watch it dissolve.

Let the ecstasy overflow and outshine the loveless self, driven mad with the torments of its self-embracing ways, hugging mightily *samsara*'s spokes of endless agony, and sing instead triumphantly with Saint Catherine, "My being is God, not by simple participation, but by a true transformation of my Being. My *me* is God!"

And let the joy sing with Dame Julian, "See! I am God! See! I am in all things! See! I do all things!" And let the joy shout with Hakuin, "This very body is the Body of Buddha! and this very land the Pure Land!"

And this Earth becomes a blessed being, and every I becomes a God, and every We becomes God's sincerest worship, and every It becomes God's most gracious temple.

And comes to rest that Godless search, tormented and tormenting. The knot in the Heart of the Kosmos relaxes to allow its only God, and overflows the Spirit ravished and enraptured by the lost and found Beloved. And gone the Godless destiny of death and desperation, and gone the madness of a life committed to uncare, and gone the tears and terror of the brutal days and endless nights where time alone would rule.

And I-I rise to taste the dawn, and find that love alone will shine today. And the Shining says: to love it all, and love it madly, and always endlessly, and ever fiercely, to love without choice and thus enter the All, to love it mindlessly and thus be the All, embracing the only and radiant Divine: now as Emptiness, now as Form, together and forever, the Godless search undone, and love alone will shine today.

[SEX, ECOLOGY, SPIRITUALITY: 522–23]

The Message of the Mystics

THE MYSTICS ASK YOU to take nothing on mere belief. Rather, they give you a set of experiments to test in your own awareness and experience. The laboratory is your own mind, the experiment is meditation. You yourself try it, and compare your test results with others who have also performed the experiment. Out of this consensually validated pool of experiential knowledge, you arrive at certain laws of the spirit—at certain "profound truths," if you will. And the first is: God is. . . .

The stunning message of the mystics is that in the very core of your being, you are God. Strictly speaking, God is neither within nor without—Spirit transcends all duality. But one discovers this by consistently looking within, until "within" becomes "beyond." The most famous version of this perennial truth occurs in the *Chandogya Upanishad,* where it says, "In this very being of yours, you do not perceive the True; but there in fact it is. In that which is the subtle essence of your own being, all that exists has its Self. An invisible and subtle essence is the Spirit of the whole universe. That is the True, that is the Self, and thou, thou art That."

Thou are That—*tat tvam asi.* Needless to say, the "thou" that is "That," the you that is God, is not your individual and isolated self or ego, this or that self, Mr. or Ms. So-and-so. In fact, the individual self or ego is precisely what blocks the realization of the Supreme Identity in the first place. Rather, the "you" in question is the deepest part of you—or, if you wish, the highest part of you— the subtle essence, as the Upanishad put it, that transcends your mortal ego and directly partakes of the Divine. In Judaism it is called the *ruach,* the divine and supraindividual spirit in each and every person, and not the *nefesh,* or the individual ego. In Christianity, it is the indwelling pneuma or spirit that is of one essence with God, and not the individual psyche or soul, which at best can worship God. As Coomaraswamy said, the distinction between a person's immortal-eternal spirit and a person's individual-mortal soul (meaning ego) is a fundamental tenet of the perennial philosophy. I think this is the only way to understand, for example, Christ's otherwise strange remarks that a person could not be a true Christian "unless he hateth his own soul." It is only by "hating" or "throwing out" or "transcending" your mortal soul that you discover your immortal spirit, one with All.

[GRACE AND GRIT: 82]

What Is Meditation?

THERE ARE MANY WAYS to explain meditation, what it is, what it does, how it works. Meditation, it is said, is a way to evoke the relaxation response. Meditation, others say, is a way to train and strengthen awareness; a method for centering and focusing the self; a way to halt constant verbal thinking and relax the body-mind; a technique for calming the central nervous system; a way to relieve stress, bolster self-esteem, reduce anxiety, and alleviate depression.

All of those are true enough; meditation has been clinically demonstrated to do all of those things. But I would like to emphasize that meditation itself is, and always has been, a *spiritual* practice. Meditation, whether Christian, Buddhist, Hindu, Taoist, or Islamic, was invented as a way for the soul to venture inward, there ultimately to find a supreme identity with Godhead. "The Kingdom of Heaven is within"—and meditation, from the very beginning, has been the royal road to that Kingdom. Whatever else it does, and it does many beneficial things, meditation is first and foremost a search for the God within.

I would say meditation is spiritual, but not religious. Spiritual has to do with actual experience, not mere beliefs; with God as the Ground of Being, not a cosmic Daddy figure; with awakening to one's true Self, not praying for one's little self; with the disciplining of awareness, not preachy and churchy moralisms about drinking and smoking and sexing; with Spirit found in everyone's Heart, not anything done in this or that church. . . .

The Essential Ken Wilber | 5

Meditation is spiritual; prayer is religious. That is, petitionary prayer, in which I ask God to give me a new car, help with my promotion, etc., is religious; it simply wishes to bolster the little ego in its wants and desires. Meditation, on the other hand, seeks to go beyond the ego altogether; it asks nothing from God, real or imagined, but rather offers itself up as a sacrifice toward a greater awareness.

Meditation, then, is not so much a part of this or that particular religion, but rather part of the universal spiritual culture of all humankind—an effort to bring awareness to bear on all aspects of life. It is, in other words, part of what has been called the perennial philosophy.

[GRACE AND GRIT: 76]

The Perennial Philosophy

THE PERENNIAL PHILOSOPHY is the worldview that has been embraced by the vast majority of the world's greatest spiritual teachers, philosophers, thinkers, and even scientists. It's called "perennial" or "universal" because it shows up in virtually all cultures across the globe and across the ages. We find it in India, Mexico, China, Japan, Mesopotamia, Egypt, Tibet, Germany, Greece. . . .

And wherever we find it, it has essentially similar features, it is in essential agreement the world over. We moderns, who can hardly agree on anything, find this rather hard to believe. But as Alan Watts summarized the available evidence: "Thus we are hardly aware of the extreme peculiarity of our own position, and find it difficult to recognize the plain fact that there has otherwise been a single philosophical consensus of universal extent. It has been held by [men and women] who report the same insights and teach the same essential doctrine whether living today or six thousand years ago, whether from New Mexico in the Far West or from Japan in the Far East."

This is really quite remarkable. I think, fundamentally, it's a testament to the universal nature of these truths, to the universal experience of a collective humanity that has everywhere agreed to certain profound truths about the human condition and about its access to the Divine. . . .

So exactly what are some of the essentials of the perennial philosophy? How many profound truths or points of agreement are there?

I'll give seven of what I think are the most important. One, Spirit exists. Two, Spirit is found within. Three, most of us don't realize this Spirit within, however, because we are living in a world of sin, separation, and duality—that is, we are living in a fallen or illusory state. Four, there is a way out of this fallen state of sin and illusion, there is a Path to our liberation. Five, if we follow this Path to its conclusion, the result is a Rebirth or Enlightenment, a *direct experience* of Spirit within, a Supreme Liberation, which—six—marks the end of sin and suffering, and which—seven—issues in social action of mercy and compassion on behalf of all sentient beings.

[GRACE AND GRIT: 77–78]

THE PERENNIAL PHILOSOPHY (the term was made famous by Huxley but coined by Leibniz)—the transcendental essence of the great religions—has as its core the notion of *advaita* or *advaya*—"nonduality," which means that reality is neither one nor many, neither permanent nor dynamic, neither separate nor unified, neither pluralistic nor holistic. It is entirely and radically above and prior to *any* form of conceptual elaboration. It is strictly unqualifiable. If it is to be discussed at all, then, as W. T. Stace so carefully pointed out, it must involve paradoxical statements. So, it is true that reality is one, but equally true that it is many; it is transcendent, but also immanent; it is prior to this world, but it is not other to this world—and so on. Sri Ramana Maharshi had a perfect summary of the paradox of the ultimate:

> The world is illusory;
> Brahman alone is real;
> Brahman is the world.

[EYE TO EYE: 153–54]

The Transpersonal

T HE WORD *transpersonal* is somewhat awkward and confuses people. But the point is simply, as Emerson put it, "The soul knows no persons." He explains (and note: Emerson throughout these quotes uses the masculine, as was the custom of the time; were he alive today he would use feminine and masculine, for the whole point of his notion of the Over-Soul was that it was neither male nor female, which is why it could anchor a true liberation from any and all restrictive roles: "The soul knows no persons"):

> Persons are supplementary to the primary teaching of the soul. In youth we are mad for persons. Childhood and youth see all the world in them. But the larger experience of man discovers the identical nature [the same self or soul] appearing through them all. In all conversation between two persons tacit reference is made, as to a third party, to a common nature. That third party or common nature is not social; it is impersonal; is God.*

The soul is without persons, and the soul is grounded in God. "Impersonal," however, is not quite right, because it tends to imply a complete negation of the personal, whereas in higher development the personal is negated and preserved, or transcended and included: hence, "transpersonal." So I think it's very important to

---

*All quotes are from *Ralph Waldo Emerson: Selected Prose and Poetry*, ed. R. Cook (San Francisco: Rinehart, 1969).

remember that *transpersonal* means "personal *plus*," not "personal minus."

But what could an actual "transpersonal" experience really mean? It's not nearly as mysterious as it sounds. At the centaur [see page 73], according to the research of Broughton (and many others), the self is *already* beginning to transcend the empirical ego or the empirical person ("the observer is distinguished from the self-concept as known"). You yourself can, right now, be aware of your objective self, you can observe your individual ego or person, you are aware of yourself generally.

But who, then, is doing the observing? What is it that is observing or witnessing your individual self? That therefore *transcends* your individual self in some important ways? Who or what is *that*? The noble Emerson:

> All goes to show that the soul in man is not an organ, but animates and exercises all the organs; is not a function, like the power of memory, of calculation, of comparison, but uses these as hands and feet; is not a faculty, but a light; is not the intellect or the will, but the master of the intellect and the will; is the background of our being, in which they lie,—an immensity not possessed and that cannot be possessed. From within or from behind, a light shines through us upon things and makes us aware that we are nothing, but the light is all.

The observer in you, the Witness in you, transcends the isolated *person* in you and opens instead—from within or from behind, as Emerson said—onto a vast expanse of awareness no longer obsessed with the individual bodymind, no longer a respecter or abuser of persons, no longer fascinated by the passing joys and set-apart sorrows of the lonely self, but standing still in silence as an opening or clearing through which light shines, not from the world but into it—"a light shines *through us* upon things." *That which* observes or witnesses the self, the person, is precisely to that degree *free* of the self, the person, and *through that opening* comes pouring the light and power of a Self, a Soul, that, as Emerson puts it, "would make our knees bend."

A man is the facade of a temple wherein all wisdom and all good abide. What we commonly call man [as an "individual person" or ego], the eating, drinking, counting man, does not, as we know him, represent himself, but misrepresents himself. Him we do not respect, but the soul, whose organ he is, if he would let it appear through his action, would make our knees bend. When it breathes through his intellect, it is genius; when it breathes through his will, it is virtue; when it flows through his affection, it is love. And the blindness of the intellect begins when it would be something of itself [be its "own person"]. The weakness of the will begins when the individual would be something of himself. All reform aims in some one particular to let the soul have its way through us. . . .

And those persons *through whom* the soul shines, *through whom* the "soul has its way," are not therefore weak characters, timid personalities, meek presences among us. They are personal plus, not personal minus. Precisely because they are no longer exclusively identified with the individual personality, and yet because they still preserve the personality, then *through that* personality flows the force and fire of the soul. They may be soft-spoken and often remain in silence, but it is a thunderous silence that veritably drowns out the egos chattering loudly all around them. Or they may be animated and very outgoing, but their dynamism is magnetic, and people are drawn somehow to the presence, fascinated. Make no mistake: these are strong characters, these souls, sometimes wildly exaggerated characters, sometimes world-historical, precisely because their personalities are plugged into a universal source that rumbles through their veins and rudely rattles those around them.

. . . [Emerson's message:] The Soul is tied to no individual, no culture, no tradition, but rises fresh in every person, beyond every person, and grounds itself in a truth and glory that bows to nothing in the world of time and place and history. We all must be, and can only be, "a light unto ourselves."

[SEX, ECOLOGY, SPIRITUALITY: 279–82]

The Essential Ken Wilber | 11

The Nondual Vision

M ANY PEOPLE HAVE stern objections to "mysticism" or "transcendentalism" of any sort, because they think it somehow denies this world, or hates this earth, or despises the body and the senses and its vital life, and so on. While that may be true of certain dissociated approaches, it is certainly not the core understanding of the great Nondual mystics, from Plotinus and Eckhart in the West to Nagarjuna and Lady Tsogyal in the East.

Rather, these sages universally maintain that absolute reality and the relative world are "not-two" (which is the meaning of "nondual"), much as a mirror and its reflections are not separate, or an ocean is one with its many waves. So the "other world" of Spirit and "this world" of separate phenomena are deeply and profoundly "not-two," and this nonduality is a direct and immediate realization which occurs in certain meditative states—in other words, seen with the eye of contemplation—although it then becomes a very simple, very ordinary perception, whether you are meditating or not. Every single thing you perceive is the radiance of Spirit itself, so much so, that Spirit is not seen apart from that thing: the robin sings, and just that is it, nothing else. This becomes your constant realization, through all changes of state, very naturally, just so. And this releases you from the basic insanity of hiding from the Real.

But why is it, then, that we ordinarily don't have that perception?

All the great Nondual wisdom traditions have given a fairly similar answer to that question. We don't see that Spirit is fully and completely present right here, right now, because our awareness is clouded with some form of avoidance. We do not want to be choicelessly aware of the present; rather, we want to run away from it, or run after it, or we want to change it, alter it, hate it, love it, loathe it, or in some way agitate to get ourselves into, or out of, it. We will do anything except come to rest in the pure Presence of the present. We will not rest with pure Presence; we want to be elsewhere, quickly. The Great Search is the game, in its endless forms.

In nondual meditation or contemplation, the agitation of the separate-self sense profoundly relaxes, and the self uncoils in the vast expanse of all space. At that point, it becomes obvious that you are not "in here" looking at the world "out there," because that duality has simply collapsed into pure Presence and spontaneous luminosity.

This realization may take many forms. A simple one is something like this: You might be looking at a mountain, and you have relaxed into the effortlessness of your own present awareness, and then suddenly the mountain is all, you are nothing. Your separate-self sense is suddenly and totally gone, and there is simply everything that is arising moment to moment. You are perfectly aware, perfectly conscious, everything seems completely normal, except you are nowhere to be found. You are not on this side of your face looking at the mountain out there; you simply are the mountain, you are the sky, you are the clouds, you are everything that is arising moment to moment, very simply, very clearly, just so.

We know all the fancy names for this state, from unity consciousness to *sahaj samadhi*. But it really is the simplest and most obvious state you will ever realize. Moreover, once you glimpse that state—what the Buddhists call One Taste (because you and the entire universe are one taste or one experience)—it becomes obvious that you are not entering this state, but rather, it is a state that, in some profound and mysterious way, has been your primordial condition from time immemorial. You have, in fact, never left this state for a second.

This is why Zen calls it the Gateless Gate: on this side of that realization, it looks like you have to do something to enter that state—it looks like you need to pass through a gate. But when you do so, and you turn around and look back, there is no gate whatsoever, and never has been. You have never left this state in the first place, so obviously you can't enter it. The gateless gate! "Every form is Emptiness just as it is," means that all things, including you and me, are always already on the other side of the gateless gate.

But if that is so, then why even do spiritual practice? Isn't that just another form of the Great Search? Yes, actually, spiritual practice is a form of the Great Search, and as such, it is destined to fail. But that is exactly the point. You and I are already convinced that there are things that we need to do in order to realize Spirit. We feel that there are places that Spirit is not (namely, in me), and we are going to correct this state of affairs. Thus, we are already committed to the Great Search, and so nondual meditation makes use of that fact and engages us in the Great Search in a particular and somewhat sneaky fashion (which Zen calls "selling water by the river").

William Blake said that "a fool who persists in his folly will become wise." So nondual meditation simply speeds up the folly. If you really think you lack Spirit, then try this folly: try to become Spirit, try to discover Spirit, try to contact Spirit, try to reach Spirit: meditate and meditate and meditate in order to get Spirit!

But of course, you see, you cannot really do this. You cannot reach Spirit any more than you can reach your feet. You always already are Spirit, you are not going to reach it in any sort of temporal thrashing around. But if this is not obvious, then try it. Nondual meditation is a serious effort to do the impossible, until you become utterly exhausted of the Great Search, sit down completely worn out, and notice your feet.

It's not that these nondual traditions deny higher states; they don't. They have many, many practices that help individuals reach specific states of postformal consciousness. But they maintain that those altered states—which have a beginning and an end in time—

ultimately have nothing to do with the timeless. The real aim is the stateless, not a perpetual fascination with changes of state. And that stateless condition is the true nature of this and every conceivable state of consciousness, so any state you have will do just fine. Change of state is not the ultimate point; recognizing the Changeless is the point, recognizing primordial Emptiness is the point, and if you are breathing and vaguely awake, that state of consciousness will do just fine.

Nonetheless, traditionally, in order to demonstrate your sincerity, you must complete a good number of preliminary practices, including a mastery of various states of meditative consciousness, summating in a stable post-postconventional adaptation, all of which is well and good. But none of those states of consciousness are held to be final or ultimate or privileged. And changing state is not the goal at all. Rather, it is precisely by entering and leaving these various meditative states that you begin to understand that *none* of them constitute enlightenment. All of them have a beginning in time, and thus none of them are the timeless. The point is to realize that change of state is *not* the point, and that realization can occur in *any* state of consciousness whatsoever.

[THE EYE OF SPIRIT: 283–86]

Of Physicists and Mystics

M Y BOOK *Quantum Questions* centered on the remarkable fact that virtually every one of the great pioneers of modern physics—men like Einstein and Schrödinger and Heisenberg—were spiritual *mystics* of one sort or another, an altogether extraordinary situation. The hardest of the sciences, physics, had run smack into the tenderest of religions, mysticism. Why? And what exactly was mysticism, anyway?

So I collected the writings of Einstein, Heisenberg, Schrödinger, Louis de Broglie, Max Planck, Niels Bohr, Wolfgang Pauli, Sir Arthur Eddington, and Sir James Jeans. The scientific genius of these men is beyond dispute (all but two were Nobel laureates); what is so amazing, as I said, is that they all shared a profoundly spiritual or mystical worldview, which is perhaps the last thing one would expect from pioneering scientists.

The essence of mysticism is that in the deepest part of your own being, in the very center of your own pure awareness, you are fundamentally one with Spirit, one with Godhead, one with the All, in a timeless and eternal and unchanging fashion. Sound far out? Listen to Erwin Schrödinger, Nobel Prize-winning cofounder of modern quantum mechanics:

"It is not possible that this unity of knowledge, feeling, and choice that you call your own should have sprung into being from nothingness at a given moment not so long ago; rather, this knowledge, feeling, and choice are essentially eternal and unchangeable and numerically one in all men, nay, in all sensitive beings. . . .

Inconceivable as it seems to ordinary reason, you—and all other conscious beings as such—are all in all. Hence this life of yours which you are living is not merely a piece of the entire existence, but is, in a certain sense, the whole. . . . This is that sacred, mystic formula which is so simple and so clear: 'I am in the east and in the west, I am above and below, *I am this whole world.*'

"Thus you can throw yourself flat on the ground, stretched out upon Mother Earth, with the certain conviction that you are one with her and she with you. You are as firmly established, as invulnerable, as she—indeed, a thousand times firmer and more invulnerable. As surely as she will engulf you tomorrow, so surely will she bring you forth anew. And not merely 'someday': now, today, every day she is bringing you forth, not once, but thousands upon thousands of times, just as every day she engulfs you a thousand times over. For eternally and always there is only now, one and the same now; the present is the only thing that has no end" [*Quantum Questions*: 97].

According to the mystics, when we go beyond or transcend our separate-self sense, our limited ego, we discover instead a Supreme Identity, an identity with the All, with universal Spirit, infinite and all-pervading, eternal and unchanging. As Einstein explains: "A human being is part of the whole, called by us 'Universe'; a part limited in time and space. He experiences himself, his thoughts and feelings as something separated from the rest—a kind of optical delusion of his consciousness. This delusion is a kind of prison for us, restricting us to our personal desires and to affection for a few persons nearest us. Our task must be to free ourselves from this prison."

Indeed, the whole point of meditation or contemplation—whether it appears in the East or in the West, whether Christian, Muslim, Buddhist, or Hindu—is to free ourselves from the "optical delusion" that we are merely separate egos set apart from each other and from eternal Spirit, and to discover instead that, once released from the prison of individuality, we are one with Godhead and thus one with all manifestation, in a perfectly timeless and eternal fashion.

And this is not a mere theoretical idea; it is a direct and immediate experience, which has been reported the world over from time immemorial, and which is essentially identical wherever it appears. As Schrödinger put it, "Within a cultural milieu where certain conceptions have been limited and specialized, it is daring to give this conclusion the simple wording that it requires. In Christian terminology to say: 'Hence I am God Almighty' sounds both blasphemous and lunatic. But please disregard these connotations for a moment, and consider that in itself, the insight is not new. In Indian thought it is considered, far from being blasphemous, to represent the quintessence of deepest insight into the happenings of the world. Again, the mystics of many centuries, independently, yet in perfect harmony with each other (somewhat like the particles in an ideal gas) have described, each of them, the unique experience of his or her life in terms that can be condensed in the phrase *Deus factus sum*—I have become God."

Not in the sense that my particular ego is God—far from it—but rather that, in the deepest part of my own awareness, I directly intersect eternity. And it was this direct intersection, this mystical awareness, that so interested these pioneering physicists.

In *Quantum Questions,* I wanted to show how and why these great physicists were all mystics, and I wanted them to be able to speak eloquently for themselves about why "the most beautiful emotion we can experience is the mystical" (Einstein), about how "the mechanism demands a mysticism" (de Broglie), about existing "in the mind of some eternal Spirit" (Jeans), about why "a synthesis embracing both rational understanding and the mystical experience of unity is the mythos, spoken or unspoken, of our present day and age" (Wolfgang Pauli), and about the most important relationship of all: "that of a human soul to a divine spirit" (Eddington).

Notice I was not saying that modern physics itself supports or proves a mystical worldview. I was saying the physicists themselves were mystics, and not that their discipline was a mystical or somehow spiritual endeavor resulting in a religious worldview. In other words, I disagreed entirely with books such as *The Tao of Physics* and *The Dancing Wu Li Masters,* which had claimed that modern physics supported or even proved Eastern mysticism.* This is a colossal error. Physics is a limited, finite, relative, and partial endeavor, dealing with a very limited aspect of reality. It does not, for example, deal with biological, psychological, economic, literary, or historical truths; whereas mysticism deals with all of that, with the Whole. To say physics proves mysticism is like saying the tail proves the dog.

To use Plato's analogy of the Cave: physics gives us a detailed picture of the shadows in the Cave (relative truth), whereas mysticism gives us a direct introduction to the Light beyond the Cave (absolute truth). Study the shadows all you want, you still won't have Light.

Moreover, none of these founding physicists believed that modern physics supports a mystical or religious worldview. They believed, rather, that modern science could no longer *object* to a religious worldview, simply because modern physics, unlike classical physics, had become acutely conscious of its extremely limited and partial role, of its total inadequacy in dealing with ultimate realities. As Eddington put it, also using Plato's analogy: "The frank realization that physical science is dealing with a world of shadows is one of the most significant of recent advances."

All of these pioneering physicists were mystics precisely because they wanted to go beyond the intrinsic limitations of physics itself to an interior and mystical awareness that, in transcending the world of shadow forms, revealed higher and more enduring realities. They were mystics, not because of physics, but in spite of physics. In other words, they wanted mysticism as meta-physics, which means "beyond physics."

And as for the attempt to support a particular religious worldview by interpretations from modern physics? Einstein, representing the majority of these physicists, called the whole attempt

---

*Fritjof Capra, the author of *The Tao of Physics* (now in a third, updated edition published by Shambhala) has since refined his views considerably; it is not so much Capra as his pale imitators, such as Gary Zukov and Fred Alan Wolf, that I have in mind.

"reprehensible." Schrödinger actually called it "sinister," and explained: "Physics has nothing to do with it. Physics takes its start from everyday experience, which it continues by more subtle means. It remains akin to it, does not transcend it generically, it cannot enter into another realm . . . because [religion's] true domain is far beyond anything in reach of scientific explanation." And Eddington was decisive: "I do not suggest that the new physics 'proves religion' or indeed gives any positive grounds for religious faith. *For my own part I am wholly opposed to any such attempt*" (italics his).

Why? Simply imagine what would happen if we indeed said that modern physics supports mysticism. What happens, for example, if we say that today's physics is in perfect agreement with Buddha's enlightenment? What happens when tomorrow's physics supplants or replaces today's physics (which it most definitely will)? Does poor Buddha then lose his enlightenment? You see the problem. If you hook your God to today's physics, then when that physics slips, that God slips with it. And *that* is what concerned these mystical physicists. They wanted neither physics distorted nor mysticism cheapened by a shotgun wedding.

[GRACE AND GRIT: 17–20]

The Real Self

THE REAL SELF has been given dozens of different names by the various mystical and metaphysical traditions throughout mankind's history. It has been known as al-Insan al-Kamil, Adam Kadmon, Ruach Adonai, Nous, Pneuma, Purusha, Tathagatagarbha, Universal Man, the Host, the Brahman-Atman, I AMness. And from a slightly different angle, it is actually synonymous with the Dharmadhatu, the Void, Suchness, and the Godhead. All of these words are simply symbols of the real world of no-boundary.

Now the real self is frequently referred to by some sort of appellation suggesting that it is the "innermost" core of humans, that it is preeminently subjective, inner, personal, non-objective, inside, and within. We are told unanimously by the mystics that "the Kingdom of Heaven is within," that we are to search the depths of our souls until we uncover, hidden in our innermost being, the Real Self of all existence. As Swami Prabhavananda used to say, "Who, what, do you think you are? Absolutely, basically, fundamentally deep within?"

One will often find the real self referred to as something like the "inner Witness," the "Absolute Seer and Knower," one's "Innermost Nature," "Absolute Subjectivity," and so on. Thus Shankara, master of Vedanta Hinduism, would say, "There is a self-existent Reality, which is the basis of our consciousness of ego. That Reality is the Witness of the three states of consciousness [waking, dreaming, sleeping], and is distinct from the five bodily coverings. That Reality is the Knower in all states of consciousness. It is aware of the presence or absence of the mind. This is Atman, the Supreme Being, the ancient." Or take this excellent quote from Zen Master Shibyama:

> It [Reality] is "Absolute Subjectivity," which transcends both subjectivity and objectivity and freely creates and uses them. It is "Fundamental Subjectivity," which can never be objectified or conceptualized and is complete in itself, with the full significance of existence in itself. To call it by these names is already a mistake, a step toward objectification and conceptualization. Master Eisai therefore remarked, "It is ever unnamable."
>
> The Absolute Subjectivity that can never be objectified or conceptualized is free from the limitations of space and time; it is not subject to life and death; it goes beyond subject and object, and although it lives in an individual, it is not restricted to the individual.

But saying that the real self is the True Seer, or Inner Witness, or Absolute Subjectivity within each of us might seem contradictory in light of what we have said thus far about unity consciousness. For, on the one hand, we have seen that the real self is an ever-present no-boundary awareness wherein the subject and the object, the seer and the seen, the experiencer and the experienced form a single continuum. Yet, on the other hand, we have just described the real self as the inner Witness, the ultimate Knower. We said it is the Seer and not the seen, it is inside and not outside. What are we to make of this seeming contradiction?

First we must recognize the difficulties the mystic faces in trying to describe the ineffable experience of unity consciousness. Foremost among these is the fact that the real self is a no-boundary awareness, whereas all our words and thoughts are nothing but boundaries. This, however, is not a flaw confined to any particular language, but is inherent in all languages by virtue of their very structure. A language possesses utility only insofar as it can construct conventional boundaries. A language of no boundaries is no language at all, and thus the mystic who tries to speak logically and formally of unity consciousness is doomed to sound very paradoxical or contradictory. The problem is that the structure of any language cannot grasp the nature of unity consciousness, any more than a fork could grasp the ocean.

So the mystics must be content with pointing and showing a Way whereby we may all experience unity consciousness for ourselves. In this sense, the mystic path is a purely experimental one. The mystics ask you to believe nothing on blind faith, to accept no authority but that of your own understanding and experience. They ask you only to try a few experiments in awareness, to look closely at your present state of existence, and to try to see your self and your world as clearly as you possibly can. Don't think, just look! as Wittgenstein exclaimed.

But just *where* to look? This is precisely the point at which the mystics universally answer, "Look inside. Deep inside. For the real self lies within." Now the mystics are not *describing* the real self as *being inside* you—they are *pointing* inside you. They are indeed saying to look within, not because the final answer actually resides within you and not without, but because as you carefully and consistently look inside, you sooner or later find outside. You realize, in other words, that the inside and the outside, the subject and the object, the seer and the seen are one, and thus you spontaneously fall into your natural state. So the mystic begins by talking of real self in a way that seems contradictory to everything we earlier said. However, if we follow the mystic through to the end, the conclusion is identical.

Start by considering what something like "Absolute Subjectivity" or "Inner Witness" might mean, at least the way the mystic uses it. Absolute Subjectivity would be that which can never, at any time, under any circumstances, be a particular object that can be seen, or heard, or known, or perceived. As the absolute Seer, it could never be seen. As the absolute Knower, it could never be known. Lao Tzu speaks of it thus:

Because the eye gazes but can catch no glimpse of it,
It is called elusive.

Because the ear listens but cannot hear it,
It is called the rarefied.
Because the hand feels for it but cannot find it,
It is called the infinitesimal.

In order to contact this real self or Absolute Subjectivity, most mystics therefore proceed with something like the following from Sri Ramana Maharshi: "The gross body which is composed of the seven humors, *I am not*; the five sense organs which apprehend their respective objects, *I am not*; even the mind which thinks, *I am not*."

But what, then, could this real self be? As Ramana pointed out, it can't be my body, because I can feel and know it, and what can be known is not the absolute Knower. It can't be my wishes, hopes, fears, and emotions, for I can to some degree see and feel them, and what can be seen is not the absolute Seer. It can't be my mind, my personality, my thoughts, for those can all be witnessed, and what can be witnessed is not the absolute Witness.

By persistently looking within for the real self in this fashion, I am, in fact, starting to realize that it cannot be found within at all. I used to think of myself as the "little subject" in here who watched all those objects out there. But the mystic shows me clearly that this "little subject" can in fact be seen as an *object*! It's not a real subject, my real self, at all.

But just here, according to the mystic, is our major problem in life and living. For most of us imagine that we can feel ourselves, or know ourselves, or perceive ourselves, or at least be aware of ourselves in some sense. We have that feeling even now. But, replies the mystic, the fact that I can see, or know, or feel my "self" at this moment shows me conclusively that this "self" cannot be my real self at all. It's a false self, a pseudo-self, an illusion and a hoax. We have inadvertently identified with a complex of *objects,* all of which we know or can know. Therefore, this complex of knowable objects cannot be the true Knower or real Self. We have identified ourselves with our body, mind, and personality, imagining these objects to constitute our real "self," and we then spend our entire lives trying to defend, protect, and prolong what is just an illusion.

We are the victims of an epidemic case of mistaken identity, with our Supreme Identity quietly but surely awaiting discovery. And the mystics want nothing more than to have us awaken to who, or what, we really and eternally are *beneath or under or prior* to our pseudo-self. Thus they ask us to cease identifying with this false self, to realize that whatever I can know, think, or feel about myself cannot constitute my real Self.

My mind, my body, my thoughts, my desires—these are no more my real Self than the trees, the stars, the clouds, and the mountains, for I can witness all of them as objects, with equal felicity. Proceeding in this fashion, I become transparent to my Self, and realize that in some sense what I am goes much, much beyond this isolated, skin-bounded organism. The more I go into I, the more I fall out of I.

As this investigation is pushed, a curious flip in consciousness occurs, which the *Lankavatara Sutra* calls "a turning about in the deepest seat of consciousness." The more I look for the absolute Seer, the more I realize that I can't find it as an object. And the simple reason I can't find it as a particular object is because it's every object! I can't feel it because it is everything felt. I can't experience it because it is everything experienced. It is true that anything I can see is *not* the Seer—because everything I see is the Seer. As I go within to find my real self, I find only the world.

But a strange thing has now happened, for I realize that the real self within is actually the real world without, and vice versa. The subject and object, the inside and outside, are and always have been nondual. There is no primary boundary. The world is my body, and what I am looking out of is what I am looking at.

Because the real self resides neither within nor without, because the subject and object are actually not-two, the mystics can speak of reality in many different but only apparently contradictory ways. They can say that in all reality there are no objects whatsoever. Or they might state that reality contains no subjects at all. Or they can deny the existence of both subject and object. Or they may speak of an Absolute Subjectivity which transcends yet includes both the relative subject and the relative object. All of these are simply various ways of saying that the inside world and the outside world are just two different names for the single, ever-present state of no-boundary awareness.

[NO BOUNDARY: 54–59]

"I-I"

THE SELF IS "not this, not that," which in Sanskrit is "*neti, neti.*" The Self is not this, not that, precisely because it is the pure Witness of this or that, and thus in all cases transcends any this and any that. The Self cannot even be said to be "One," for that is just another quality, another object that is perceived or witnessed. The Self is not "Spirit"; rather, it is that which, right now, is witnessing that concept. The Self is not the "Witness"—that is just another word or concept, and the Self is that which is witnessing that concept. The Self is not Emptiness, the Self is not a pure Self—and so on.

> There are neither good nor bad qualities in the Self. The Self is free from all qualities. Qualities pertain to the mind only. It is beyond quality. If there is unity, there will also be duality. The numerical one gives rise to other numbers. The truth is neither one nor two. It is as it is.

> People want to see the Self as something. They desire to see it as a blazing light, etc. But how could that be? The Self is not light, not darkness, not any observed thing. The Self is ever the Witness. It is eternal and remains the same all along.*

Ramana Maharshi often refers to the Self by the name "I-I," since the Self is the simple Witness of even the ordinary "I." We

---

*All quotes are from *Talks with Sri Ramana Maharshi* (Tiruvannamalai: Sri Ramanasramam, 1984).

are all, says Ramana, perfectly aware of the I-I, for we are all aware of our capacity to witness in the present moment. But we *mistake* the pure I-I or pure Seer with some sort of object *that can be seen* and is thus precisely not the Seer or the true Self, but is merely some sort of memory or image or identity or self-concept, all of which are objects, none of which is the Witness of objects. We identify the I-I with this or that I, and thus identified with a mere finite and temporal object, we suffer the slings and arrows of all finite objects, whereas the Self remains ever as it is, timeless, eternal, unborn, unwavering, undying, ever and always present.

The I-I is always there. There is no knowing it [as an object]. It is not a new knowledge acquired. The I-I is always there.

There is no one who even for a trice fails to experience the Self. In deep sleep you exist; awake, you remain. The same Self is in both states. The difference is only in the awareness and the non-awareness of the world. The world rises with the mind and sets with the mind. That which rises and sets is not the Self.

The individual is miserable because he confounds the mind and body with the Self. It is the nature of the mind to wander. But you are not the mind. The mind springs up and sinks down. It is impermanent, transitory, whereas you are eternal. There is nothing but the Self. To abide as the Self is the thing. Never mind the mind. If the mind's source is sought, the mind will vanish leaving the Self unaffected.

. . . Ramana therefore counsels us to seek the *source* of the mind, to look for that which is aware of the mental or personal "I," for *that* is the transpersonal "I-I," unchanged by the fluctuations of any particular states, particular objects, particular circumstances, particular births, particular deaths.

Tracing the source of "I," the primal I-I alone remains over, and it is inexpressible. The seat of Realization is within and the seeker cannot find it as an object outside him. That seat is bliss and is the core [the ultimate depth] of all beings. Hence it is called the Heart. The mind now sees itself diversified as the universe. If the diversity is not manifest it remains in its own essence, its original state, and that is the Heart. Entering the Heart means remaining without distractions [objects]. The Heart is the only Reality. The mind is only a transient phase. To remain as one's Self is to enter the Heart.

The Self is not born nor does it die. The sages see everything in the Self. There is no diversity in it. If a man thinks that he is born and cannot avoid the fear of death, let him find out if the Self has any birth. He will discover that the Self always exists, that the body which is born resolves itself into thought and that the emergence of thought is the root of all mischief. Find the source of thoughts. Then you will abide in the ever-present inmost Self and be free from the idea of birth and the fear of death.

As one pursues this "self-inquiry" into the source of thoughts, into the source of "I" and the "world," one enters a state of pure empty awareness, free of all objects whatsoever, . . . which in Vedanta is known as *nirvikalpa samadhi* (*nirvikalpa* means "without any qualities or objects"). In awareness, there is perfect clarity, perfect consciousness, but the entire manifest world (up to and including the subtle) simply *ceases to arise,* and one is directly introduced to what Meister Eckhart called "the naked existence of Godhead." Sri Ramana:

If you hold to the Self [remain as Witness in all circumstances], there is no second. When you see the world you have lost hold of the Self. On the contrary, hold the Self and the world will not appear.

By unswerving vigilant constancy in the Self, ceaseless like the unbroken flow of water, is generated the natural or changeless state of *nirvikalpa samadhi*, which readily and spontaneously yields that direct, immediate, unobstructed and universal perception of Brahman, which transcends all time and space.

For Ramana and Eckhart (and not them alone), the causal is a type of ultimate omega point. As the *Source* of all manifestation, it is the Goal of all development. Ramana: "This is Self-Realization; and thereby is cut asunder the Knot of the Heart [the separate-self sense]; this is the limitless bliss of liberation, beyond doubt and duality. To realize this state of freedom from duality is *the summum bonum* of life: and he alone that has won it is a *jivanmukta* (the liberated one while yet alive), and not he who has merely a theoretical understanding of the Self or the desired end and aim of all human behavior. The disciple is then enjoined to remain in the beatitude of Aham-Brahman—'I-I' is the Absolute."

[Sex, Ecology, Spirituality: 306–308]

Egolessness

PRECISELY BECAUSE the ego, the soul, and the Self can all be present simultaneously, we can better understand the real meaning of "egolessness," a notion that has caused an inordinate amount of confusion. But egolessness does not mean the absence of a functional self (that's a psychotic, not a sage); it means that one is no longer exclusively identified with that self.

One of the many reasons we have trouble with the notion of "egoless" is that people want their "egoless sages" to fulfill all their fantasies of "saintly" or "spiritual," which usually means dead from the neck down, without fleshy wants or desires, gently smiling all the time. All of the things that people typically have trouble with—money, food, sex, relationships, desire—they want their saints to be without. "Egoless sages" are "above all that," is what people want. Talking heads is what they want. Religion, they believe, will simply get rid of all baser instincts, drives, and relationships, and hence they look to religion, not for advice on how to live life with enthusiasm, but on how to avoid it, repress it, deny it, escape it.

In other words, the typical person wants the spiritual sage to be "less than a person," somehow devoid of all the messy, juicy, complex, pulsating, desiring, urging forces that drive most human beings. We expect our sages to be an *absence* of all that drives *us*! All the things that frighten us, confuse us, torment us, confound us: we want our sages to be untouched by them altogether. And that absence, that vacancy, that "less than personal," is what we often mean by "egoless."

But "egoless" does not mean "*less* than personal"; it means "*more* than personal." Not personal minus, but personal plus—all the normal personal qualities, *plus* some transpersonal ones. Think of the great yogis, saints, and sages—from Moses to Christ to Padmasambhava. They were not feeble-mannered milquetoasts, but fierce movers and shakers—from bullwhips in the Temple to subduing entire countries. They rattled the world on its own terms, not in some pie-in-the-sky piety; many of them instigated massive social revolutions that have continued for thousands of years. And they did so, not because they avoided the physical, emotional, and mental dimensions of humanness, and the ego that is their vehicle, but because they engaged them with a drive and intensity that shook the world to its very foundations. No doubt, they were also plugged into the soul (deeper psychic) and spirit (formless Self)—the ultimate source of their power—but they expressed that power, and gave it concrete results, precisely because they dramatically engaged the lower dimensions through which that power could speak in terms that could be heard by all.

These great movers and shakers were not small egos; they were, in the very best sense of the term, big egos, precisely because the ego (the functional vehicle of the gross realm) can and does exist alongside the soul (the vehicle of the subtle) and the Self (vehicle of the causal). To the extent these great teachers *moved the gross realm*, they did so with their egos, because the ego is the functional vehicle of that realm. They were not, however, identified merely with their egos (that's a narcissist); they simply found their egos plugged into a radiant Kosmic source. The great yogis, saints, and sages accomplished so much precisely because they were not timid little toadies but great big egos, plugged into the dynamic Ground and Goal of the Kosmos itself, plugged into their own higher Self, alive to the pure Atman (the pure I-I) that is one with Brahman; they opened their mouths and the world trembled, fell to its knees, and confronted its radiant God.

Saint Teresa was a great contemplative? Yes, *and* Saint Teresa is the only woman ever to have reformed an entire Catholic monastic tradition (think about it). Gautama Buddha shook India to its foundations. Rumi, Plotinus, Bodhidharma, Lady Tsogyal, Lao Tzu, Plato, the Baal Shem Tov—these men and women started revolutions in the gross realm that lasted hundreds, sometimes thousands, of years, something neither Marx nor Lenin nor Locke nor Jefferson can yet claim. And they did not do so because they were dead from the neck down. No, they were monumentally, gloriously, divinely big egos, plugged into a deeper psychic, which was plugged straight into God.

There is certainly a type of truth to the notion of *transcending ego*: it doesn't mean destroy the ego, it means plug it into something bigger. As Nagarjuna put it, in the relative world, *atman* is real; in the absolute, neither *atman* nor *anatman* is real. Thus, in neither case is *anatta* a correct description of reality. The small ego does not evaporate; it remains as the functional center of activity in the conventional realm. As I said, to lose that ego is to become a psychotic, not a sage.

"Transcending the ego" thus actually means to *transcend but include* the ego in a deeper and higher embrace, first in the soul or deeper psychic, then with the Witness or primordial Self, then with each previous stage taken up, enfolded, included, and embraced in the radiance of One Taste. And that means we do not "get rid" of the small ego, but rather, we inhabit it fully, live it with verve, use it as the necessary vehicle through which higher truths are communicated. Soul and Spirit include body, emotions, and mind; they do not erase them.

Put bluntly, the ego is not an obstruction to Spirit, but a radiant manifestation of Spirit. All Forms are not other than Emptiness, including the form of the ego. It is not necessary to get rid of the ego, but simply to live with it a certain exuberance. When identification spills out of the ego and into the Kosmos at large, the ego discovers that the individual Atman is in fact all of a piece with Brahman. The big Self is indeed *no small ego,* and thus, to the extent you are stuck in your small ego, a death and transcendence is required. Narcissists are simply people whose egos are not yet big enough to embrace the entire Kosmos, and so they try to be central to the Kosmos instead.

But we do not want our sages to have big egos; we do not even want them to display a manifest dimension at all. Anytime a sage displays humanness—in regard to money, food, sex, relationships—we are shocked, *shocked*, because we are planning to escape life altogether, not live it, and the sage who lives life offends us. We want out, we want to ascend, we want to escape, and the sage who engages life with gusto, lives it to the hilt, grabs each wave of life and surfs it to the end—this deeply, profoundly disturbs us, frightens us, because it means that we, too, might have to engage life, with gusto, on all levels, and not merely escape it in a cloud of luminous ether. We do not want our sages to have bodies, egos, drives, vitality, sex, money, relationships, or life, because those are what habitually torture us, and we want out. We do not want to surf the waves of life, we want the waves to go away. We want vaporware spirituality.

The integral sage, the nondual sage, is here to show us otherwise. Known generally as "Tantric," these sages insist on transcending life by living it. They insist on finding release by engagement, finding nirvana in the midst of *samsara*, finding total liberation by complete immersion. They enter with awareness the nine rings of hell, for nowhere else are the nine heavens found. Nothing is alien to them, for there is nothing that is not One Taste.

Indeed, the whole point is to be fully at home in the body and its desires, the mind and its ideas, the spirit and its light. To embrace them fully, evenly, simultaneously, since all are equally gestures of the One and Only Taste. To inhabit lust and watch it play; to enter ideas and follow their brilliance; to be swallowed by Spirit and awaken to a glory that time forgot to name. Body and mind and spirit, all contained, equally contained, in the ever-present awareness that grounds the entire display.

In the stillness of the night, the Goddess whispers. In the brightness of the day, dear God roars. Life pulses, mind imagines, emotions wave, thoughts wander. What are all these but the endless movements of One Taste, forever at play with its own gestures, whispering quietly to all who would listen: is this not you yourself?

When the thunder roars, do you not hear your Self? When the lightning cracks, do you not see your Self? When clouds float quietly across the sky, is this not your very own limitless Being, waving back at you?

[ONE TASTE: November 17]

The Witness Exercise

The Witness Exercise is a summary of some of the ways that the world's mystics have used to move beyond body and mind and find instead the inner witness, the transcendent self. Wilber says, "This particular version I adapted from Roberto Assagioli, founder of Psychosynthesis, but it's a standard technique of self-inquiry—the primordial inquiry 'Who am I?'—perhaps made most famous by Sri Ramana Maharshi."

NOTICE FIRST OF ALL the broad, distinguishing marks of the transcendent self: it is a center and expanse of awareness which is creatively detached from one's personal mind, body, emotions, thoughts, and feelings. So if you would like to begin to work at intuiting this transcendent self within you that goes beyond you, the you that is not you, then proceed as follows:

Begin with two or three minutes of centaur awareness [see "Healing the Bodymind Split," page 75] (for the simple reason that you will then be more or less in touch with the centaur level, and that much "closer" to the transpersonal bands beneath it). Then, slowly begin to silently recite the following to yourself, trying to realize as vividly as possible the import of each statement:

I *have* a body, but I am *not* my body. I can see and feel my body, and what can be seen and felt is not the true Seer. My body may be tired or excited, sick or healthy, heavy or light, but that has nothing to do with my inward I. I *have* a body, but I am *not* my body.

I *have* desires, but I am *not* my desires. I can know my desires, and what can be known is not the true Knower. Desires come and go, floating through my awareness, but they do not affect my inward I. *I have* desires but I am *not* desires.

I *have* emotions, but I am *not* my emotions. I can feel and sense my emotions, and what can be felt and sensed is not the true Feeler. Emotions pass through me, but they do not affect my inward I. I *have* emotions but I am *not* emotions.

I *have* thoughts, but I am *not* my thoughts. I can know and intuit my thoughts, and what can be known is not the true Knower. Thoughts come to me and thoughts leave me, but they do not affect my inward I. I *have* thoughts but I am *not* my thoughts.

This done—perhaps several times—one then affirms as concretely as possible: I am what remains, a pure center of awareness, an unmoved witness of all these thoughts, emotions, feelings, and desires.

If you persist at such an exercise, the understanding contained in it will quicken and you might begin to notice fundamental changes in your sense of "self." For example, you might begin intuiting a deep inward sense of freedom, lightness, release, stability. This source, this "center of the cyclone," will retain its lucid stillness even amid the raging winds of anxiety and suffering that might swirl around its center. The discovery of this witnessing center is very much like diving from the calamitous waves on the surface of a stormy ocean to the quiet and secure depths of the bottom. At first you might not get more than a few feet beneath the agitated waves of emotion, but with persistence you may gain the ability to dive fathoms into the quiet depths of your soul, and lying outstretched at the bottom, gaze up in alert but detached fashion *at* the turmoil that once held you transfixed.

Here we are talking of the transpersonal self or witness—we are not discussing pure unity consciousness. In unity consciousness, the transpersonal witness itself collapses into everything witnessed. Before that can occur, however, one must first discover that transpersonal witness, which then acts as an easier "jumping-off point" for unity consciousness. And we find this transpersonal witness by dis-identifying with *all* particular objects, mental, emotional, or physical, thereby transcending them.

To the extent that you actually realize that you are not, for example, your anxieties, then your anxieties no longer threaten you. Even if anxiety is present, it no longer overwhelms you because you are no longer exclusively tied to it. You are no longer courting it, fighting it, resisting it, or running from it. In the most radical fashion, anxiety is thoroughly accepted as it is and allowed to move as it will. You have nothing to lose, nothing to gain, by its presence or absence, for you are simply watching it pass by.

Thus, any emotion, sensation, thought, memory, or experience that disturbs you is simply one with which you have exclusively identified yourself, and the ultimate resolution of the disturbance is simply to *dis-identify* with it. You cleanly let all of them drop away by realizing that they are not you—since you can see them, they cannot be the true Seer and Subject. Since they are not your real self, there is no reason whatsoever for you to identify with them, hold on to them, or allow your self to be bound by them.

Slowly, gently, as you pursue this dis-identification "therapy," you may find that your entire *individual* self (persona, ego, centaur), which heretofore you have fought to defend and protect, begins to go transparent and drop away. Not that it literally falls off and you find yourself floating, disembodied, through space. Rather, you begin to feel that what happens to your personal self— your wishes, hopes, desires, hurts—is not a matter of life-or-death seriousness, because there is within you a deeper and more basic self which is not touched by these peripheral fluctuations, these surface waves of grand commotion but feeble substance.

Thus, your personal mind-and-body may be in pain, or humiliation, or fear, but as long as you abide as the witness of these affairs, as if from on high, they no longer threaten you, and thus you are no longer moved to manipulate them, wrestle with them, or subdue them. Because you are willing to witness them, to look at them impartially, you are able to transcend them. As St. Thomas put it, "Whatever knows certain things cannot have any of them in its own nature." Thus, if the eye were colored red, it wouldn't be able to perceive red objects. It can see red because it is clear, or "red-less." Likewise, if we can but watch or witness our distresses, we prove ourselves thereby to be "distress-less," free of the witnessed turmoil. That within which feels pain is itself pain-less; that which feels fear is fear-less; that which perceives tension is tension-less. To witness these states is to transcend them. They no longer seize you from behind because you look at them up front.

Thus, we can understand why Patanjali, the codifier of yoga in India, said that ignorance is the identification of the Seer with the instruments of seeing. Every time we become exclusively identified with or attached to the persona, ego, body, or centaur, then anything which threatens their existence or standards seems to threaten our very Self. Thus, every attachment to thoughts, sensations, feelings, or experiences is merely another link in the chain of our own self-enslavement. . . .

As we begin to touch the transpersonal witness, we begin to let go of our purely personal problems, worries, and concerns. In fact, we don't even try to solve our problems or distresses, as we surely would and should on the persona, ego, or centaur levels. For our only concern here is to *watch* our particular distresses, to simply and innocently be aware of them, without judging them, avoiding them, dramatizing them, working on them, or justifying them. As a feeling or tendency arises, we witness it. If hatred of that feeling arises, we witness that. If hatred of the hatred arises, then we witness that. Nothing is to be done, but if a doing arises, we witness that. Abide as "choiceless awareness" in the midst of all distresses. This is possible only when we understand that none of them constitute our real self. As long as we are attached to them, there will be an effort, however subtle, to manipulate them. Understanding that they are not the center or self, we don't call our distresses names, yell at them, resent them, try to reject them or indulge them. Every move we make to solve a distress simply reinforces the illusion that we are that particular distress. Thus, ultimately to try to escape a distress merely perpetuates that distress. What is so upsetting is not the distress itself, but our *attachment* to that distress. We identify with it, and that alone is the real difficulty.

Instead of fighting a distress, we simply assume the innocence of a detached impartiality toward it. The mystics and sages are fond of likening this state of witnessing to a mirror. We simply reflect any sensations or thoughts that arise without clinging to them or pushing them away, just as a mirror perfectly and impartially reflects whatever passes in front of it. Says Chuang Tzu, "The perfect person employs the mind as a mirror. It grasps nothing; it refuses nothing; it receives, but does not keep."

If you are at all successful in developing this type of detached witnessing (it does take time), you will be able to look upon the events occurring in your mind-and-body with the very same impartiality that you would look upon clouds floating through the sky, water rushing in a stream, rain cascading on a roof, or any other objects in your field of awareness. In other words, your *relationship* to your mind-and-body becomes the same as your *relationship* to *all other objects*. Heretofore, you have been using your mind-and-body as something with which to look at the world. Thus, you became intimately attached to them and bound to their limited perspective. You became identified exclusively with them and thus you were tied and bound to their problems, pains, and distresses. But by persistently looking at them, you realize they are merely *objects* of awareness—in fact, objects of the transpersonal witness. "I *have* a mind and body and emotions, but I am *not* a mind and body and emotions."

[NO BOUNDARY: 128–32]

Levels of Consciousness

THE MOST STRIKING FEATURE of the perennial philosophy/psychology is that it presents being and consciousness as a hierarchy of dimensional levels, moving from the lowest, densest, and most fragmentary realms to the highest, subtlest, and most unitary ones. In Hinduism, for example, the lowest level is called the *annamayakosha,* which means the level made of food—that is, the physical body and the material cosmos. The next level is *pranamayakosha*—the sheath made of biological functions, life-breath, emotions, bioenergy, and so on. Both of these levels, in Mahayana Buddhism, are referred to as the five *vijñanas*—the realm of the five senses and their physical objects.

The next highest level, according to Hinduism, is the *manomayakosha,* "the sheath made of mind." In Buddhism, this is called the *manovijñana*—the mind that stays (myopically) close to the five senses. This is approximately the level we in the West would call intellect, mind, mental-ego, secondary process, operational thinking, and so on.

Beyond conventional mind, according to Hinduism, is the *vijñanamayakosha* (what Buddhists call *manas*). This is a very high form of mind, so high, in fact, that it is better to refer to it by a different name—the most common being "the subtle realm." The subtle is said to include archetypal processes, high-order insights and visions, ecstatic intuition, an extraordinary clarity of awareness, an open ground-consciousness that reaches far beyond the ordinary ego, mind, and body.

Beyond the subtle lies the causal realm (Hinduism: *anandamay-akosha*; Buddhism: tainted *alayavijñana*). This is a realm of perfect transcendence, so perfect that it is said to reach beyond the conception, experience, and imagination of any ordinary individual. It is a realm of formless Radiance, of radical insight into all of manifestation, blissful release into infinity, the breaking of all boundaries, high or low, and of absolutely panoramic or perfectly mirrorlike wisdom and awareness.

Passing through the causal realm, consciousness reawakens to its absolute abode. This is Consciousness as Such, and not only is it the infinite limit of the spectrum of being, it is the nature, source, and suchness of each level of the spectrum. It is radically all-pervading, one without a second. At this point—but not before—all levels are seen to be perfect and equal manifestations of this ultimate Mystery. There are then no levels, no dimensions, no higher, no lower, no sacred, no profane, so matter-of-factly so that Zen describes it thus:

> As the wind sways the willows
> Velvet beads move in the air.
> As the rain falls on the pear blossoms
> White butterflies lilt in the sky.

The above summary would give us approximately six major levels—physical, biological, mental, subtle, causal, and ultimate (listed below). Now many traditions greatly subdivide and extend this model (the subtle, for instance, is said to consist of seven levels). But aside from that, it is important to understand that all major perennial traditions agree with that general hierarchy, and most of them agree right down to details. Further, this hierarchy is not a nicety of philosophical side issues; for these traditions, it is the fundamental core of the perennial wisdom insofar as it can be stated in words. It is fair to say, then, that any account of the mystic's "worldview" that leaves out this type of hierarchy is seriously inadequate.

According to the perennial traditions, each of these various levels has an appropriate field of study. The study of level-1 is basically that of physics and chemistry, the study of nonliving things. Level-2 is the realm of biology, the study of life processes. Level-3 is the level of both psychology (when awareness is "turned in") and philosophy (when it is "turned out"). Level-4, the subtle, is the realm of saintly religion; that is, religion which aims for visionary insight, halos of light and bliss, angelic or archetypal intuition, and so on. Level-5, the causal, is the realm of sagely religion, which aims not so much for higher experiences as for the dissolution and transcendence of the experiencer. This sagely path involves the transcendence of all subject-object duality in formless consciousness. Level-6, the ultimate, awaits any who push through the final barriers of levels 4 and 5 so as to radically awaken as ultimate consciousness.

1. Physical: nonliving matter/energy
2. Biological: living, sentient matter/energy
3. Psychological: mind, ego, logic, thinking
4. Subtle: archetypal, transindividual, intuitive
5. Causal: formless radiance, perfect transcendence
6. Ultimate: consciousness as such, the source and nature of all other levels

[EYE TO EYE: 124–26]

Constant Consciousness

I BECAME EXTREMELY SERIOUS about meditation practice when I read the following line from the illustrious Sri Ramana Maharshi: "That which is not present in deep dreamless sleep is not real."

That is a shocking statement, because basically, there is nothing—literally nothing—in the deep dreamless state. That was his point. Ultimate reality (or Spirit), Ramana said, cannot be something that pops into consciousness and then pops out. It must be something that is constant, permanent, or, more technically, something that, being *timeless,* is *fully present* at every point in time. Therefore, ultimate reality must also be fully present in deep dreamless sleep, and anything that is *not* present in deep dreamless sleep is *not* ultimate reality.

This profoundly disturbed me, because I had had several *kensho* or *satori*-like experiences (powerful glimpses of One Taste), but they were all confined to the waking state. Moreover, most of the things I cared for existed in the waking state. And yet clearly the waking state is not permanent. It comes and goes every twenty-four hours. And yet, according to the great sages, there is something in us that is *always conscious*—that is literally conscious or aware at all times and through all states, waking, dreaming, sleeping. And that *ever-present awareness is Spirit* in us. That underlying current of constant consciousness (or nondual awareness) is a direct and unbroken ray of pure Spirit itself. It is our connection with the Goddess, our pipeline straight to God.

Thus, if we want to realize our supreme identity with Spirit, we will have to plug ourselves into this current of constant consciousness, and follow it through all changes of state-waking, dreaming, sleeping—which will (1) strip us of an exclusive identification with any of those states (such as the body, the mind, the ego, or the soul); and (2) allow us to recognize and identify with that which is constant—or timeless—through all of those states, namely, Consciousness as Such, by any other name, timeless Spirit. . . .

The moment this constant nondual consciousness is obvious in your case, a new destiny will awaken in the midst of the manifest world. You will have discovered your own Buddha-mind, your own Godhead, your own formless, spaceless, timeless, infinite Emptiness, your own Atman that is Brahman, your Keter, Christ consciousness, radiant Shekhinah—in so many words, One Taste. It is unmistakably so. And just that is your true identity—pure Emptiness or pure unqualifiable Consciousness as Such—and thus you are released from the terror and the torment that necessarily arise when you identify with a little subject in a world of little objects.

Once you find your formless identity as Buddha-mind, as Atman, as pure Spirit or Godhead, you will take that constant, nondual, ever-present consciousness and re-enter the lesser states, subtle mind and gross body, and re-animate them with radiance. You will not remain merely Formless and Empty. You will Empty yourself of Emptiness: you will pour yourself out into the mind and world, and create them in the process, and enter them all equally, but especially and particularly that specific mind and body that is called you (that is called, in my case, Ken Wilber); this lesser self will become the vehicle of the Spirit that you are.

And then all things, including your own little mind and body and feelings and thoughts, will arise in the vast Emptiness that you are, and they will self-liberate into their own true nature just as they arise, precisely because you no longer identify with any one of them, but rather let them play, let them all arise, in the Emptiness and Openness that you now are. You then will awaken as radical Freedom, and sing those songs of radiant release, beam an infinity too obvious to see, and drink an ocean of delight. You will look at the moon as part of your body and bow to the sun as part of your heart, and it is all just so. For eternally and always, eternally and always, there is only *this*.

But you have not found this Freedom, or in any way attained it. It is in fact the same Freedom that has lived in the house of the pure Witness from the very start. You are merely recognizing the pure and empty Self, the radical I-I, that has been your natural awareness from the beginning and all along, but that you didn't notice because you had become lost in the intoxicating movie of life.

With the awakening of constant consciousness, you become something of a divine schizophrenic, in the popular sense of "split-minded," because you have access to *both* the Witness and the ego. You are actually "whole-minded," but it sounds like it's split, because you are aware of the constant Witness or Spirit in you, and you are also perfectly aware of the movie of life, the ego and all its ups and downs. So you still feel pain and suffering and sorrow, but they can no longer convince you of their importance—you are no longer the victim of life, but its Witness.

In fact, because you are no longer afraid of your feelings, you can engage them with much greater intensity. The movie of life becomes more vivid and vibrant, precisely because you are no longer grasping or avoiding it, and thus no longer trying to dull or dilute it. You no longer turn the volume down. You might even cry harder, laugh louder, jump higher. Choiceless awareness doesn't mean you cease to feel; it means you feel fully, feel deeply, feel to infinity itself, and laugh and cry and love until it hurts. Life jumps right off the screen, and you are one with all of it, because you don't recoil.

If you are having a dream, and you think it's real, it can get very scary. Say you are dreaming that you are tightrope-walking across Niagara Falls. If you fall off, you plunge to your death. So you are walking very slowly, very carefully. Then suppose you start lucid dreaming, and you realize that it's just a dream. What do you do? Become more cautious and careful? No, you start jumping up and down on the tightrope, you do flips, you bounce around, you have a ball—precisely because you know it isn't real. When you realize it's a dream, you can afford to play.

The same thing happens when you realize that ordinary life is just a dream, just a movie, just a play. You don't become more cautious, more timid, more reserved. You start jumping up and down and doing flips, precisely because it's all a dream, it's all pure Emptiness. You don't feel less, you feel more—because you can afford to. You are no longer afraid of dying, and therefore you are not afraid of living. You become radical and wild, intense and vivid, shocking and silly. You let it all come pouring through, because it's all your dream.

Life then assumes its true intensity, its vivid luminosity, its radical effervescence. Pain is more painful and happiness is happier; joy is more joyous and sorrow is even sadder. It all comes radiantly alive to the mirror-mind, the mind that doesn't grasp or avoid, that simply witnesses the play, and therefore can afford to play, even as it watches.

What would motivate you if you saw everything as the dream of your own highest Self? What would actually move you in this playful dream world? Everything in the dream is basically fun, at some deep level, except for this: when you see your friends suffering because they think the dream is real, you want to relieve their suffering, you want them to wake up, too. Watching them suffer is not fun. And so a deep and powerful compassion arises in the heart of the awakened ones, and they seek, above all else, to awaken others—and thus relieve them from the sorrow and the pity, the torment and the pain, the terror and the anguish that come from taking with dreadful seriousness the silly dream of life.

So you are a divine schizophrenic, you are "split-minded" in the sense that you are simultaneously in touch with both the pure Witness and the world of the ego-film. But that really means you are actually "whole-minded," because these two worlds are really not-two. The ego is just the dream of the Witness, the film that the Witness creates out of its own infinite plenitude, simply so it will have something to watch at the movies.

At that point the entire play arises within your own constant consciousness. There is no inside and no outside, no in here versus out there. The nondual universe of One Taste arises as a spontaneous gesture of your own true nature. You can taste the sun and swallow the moon, and centuries fit in the palm of your hand. The pure I-I, the great I AMness, breathes to infinity and creates a Kosmos as the Song of its very Self, and oceans of compassion fall as tears from your very own Original Face.

Last night I saw the reflection of the moon in a cool clear crystal pond, and nothing else happened at all.

[ONE TASTE: March 23–24]

The Great Chain of Being

CENTRAL TO THE perennial philosophy is the notion of the *Great Chain of Being*. The idea itself is fairly simple. Reality, according to the perennial philosophy, is not one-dimensional; it is not a flatland of uniform substance stretching monotonously before the eye. Rather, reality is composed of several *different but continuous* dimensions. Manifest reality, that is, consists of different grades or levels, reaching from the lowest and most dense and least conscious to the highest and most subtle and most conscious. At one end of this continuum of being or spectrum of consciousness is what we in the West would call "matter" or the insentient and the nonconscious, and at the other end is "spirit" or "Godhead" or the "superconscious" (which is also said to be the all-pervading ground of the entire sequence). Arrayed in between are the other dimensions of being, arranged according to their individual degrees of reality (Plato), actuality (Aristotle), inclusiveness (Hegel), consciousness (Aurobindo), clarity (Leibniz), embrace (Plotinus), or knowingness (Garab Dorje).

Sometimes the Great Chain is presented as having just three major levels: matter, mind, and spirit. Other versions give five levels: matter, body, mind, soul, and spirit. Still others give very exhaustive breakdowns of the Great Chain; some of the yogic systems give literally dozens of discrete yet continuous dimensions. For the time being, our simple hierarchy of matter to body to mind to soul to spirit will suffice.

The central claim of the perennial philosophy is that *men and women can grow and develop (or evolve) all the way up the hierarchy to Spirit itself,* therein to realize a "supreme identity" with Godhead—the *ens perfectissimum* toward which all growth and evolution yearns.

But before we get to that, the first thing that we can't help but notice is that the Great Chain is indeed a "hierarchy"—a word that has fallen on very hard times. . . . But as used by the perennial philosophy—and indeed, as used in modern psychology, evolutionary theory, and systems theory—a hierarchy is simply a ranking of orders of events *according to their holistic capacity.* In any developmental sequence, what is whole at one stage becomes merely part of a larger whole at the next stage. A letter is part of a whole word, which is part of a whole sentence, which is part of a whole paragraph, and so on. Arthur Koestler coined the term "holon" to refer to that which, being a whole in one context, is a part of a wider whole in another. With reference to the phrase "the bark of a dog," for example, the word "bark" is a whole with reference to its individual letters, but a part with reference to the phrase itself. And the whole (or the context) can determine the meaning and function of a part—the meaning of "bark" is different in the phrases "the bark of a dog" and "the bark of a tree." The whole, in other words, is more than the sum of its parts, and that whole can influence and determine, in many cases, the function of its parts.

Hierarchy, then, is simply an order of increasing holons, representing an increase in wholeness and integrative capacity. This is why hierarchy is so central to systems theory, the theory of wholeness or holism ("wholism"). And it is absolutely central to the perennial philosophy. Each expanding link in the Great Chain of Being represents an increase in unity and wider identities, from the isolated identity of the body through the social and communal identity of the mind to the supreme identity of Spirit, an identity with literally all manifestation. This is why the great hierarchy of being is often drawn as a series of concentric circles or spheres or "nests within nests." [So] the Great Chain is actually the Great Nest of Being.

And finally, hierarchy is asymmetrical (or a "higher"-archy) because the process does not occur in the reverse. For example, there are first letters, then words, then sentences, then paragraphs, but not vice versa. And that "not vice versa" constitutes an unavoidable hierarchy or ranking or asymmetrical order of increasing wholeness.

. . . As I said, all of the world's great wisdom traditions are basically variations of the perennial philosophy, of the Great Holarchy of Being. In his wonderful book *Forgotten Truth,* Huston Smith summarizes the world's major religions in one phrase: "a hierarchy of being and knowing." Chögyam Trungpa Rinpoche pointed out, in *Shambhala: The Sacred Path of the Warrior,* that the essential and background idea pervading all of the philosophies of the East, from India to Tibet to China, lying behind everything from Shintoism to Taoism, is "a hierarchy of earth, human, heaven," which he also pointed out is equivalent to "body, mind, spirit." And Coomaraswamy noted that the world's great religions, bar none, "in their different degrees represent a hierarchy of types or levels of consciousness extending from animal to deity, and according to which one and the same individual may function on different occasions."

Which brings us to the most notorious paradox in the perennial philosophy. We have seen that the wisdom traditions subscribe to the notion that reality manifests in levels or dimensions, with each higher dimension being more inclusive and therefore "closer" to the absolute totality of Godhead or Spirit. In this sense, Spirit is the summit of being, the highest rung on the ladder of evolution. But it is also true that Spirit is *the wood out of which the entire ladder and all its rungs are made.* Spirit is the suchness, the isness, the essence of each and every thing that exists.

The first aspect, the highest-rung aspect, is the *transcendental* nature of Spirit—it far surpasses any "worldly" or creaturely or finite things. The entire earth (or even universe) could be destroyed, and Spirit would remain. The second aspect, the wood aspect, is the im*manent* nature of Spirit—Spirit is equally and totally present in all manifest things and events, in nature, in culture, in heaven and on earth, with no partiality. From this angle, no phenomenon whatsoever is closer to Spirit than another, for all are equally "made of" Spirit. Thus, Spirit is *both* the highest *goal* of all development and evolution, and the *ground* of the entire sequence, as present fully at the beginning as at the end. Spirit is prior to this world, but not other to this world.

Failure to take both of those paradoxical aspects of Spirit into account has historically led to some very lopsided (and politically dangerous) views of Spirit. Traditionally, the patriarchal religions have tended to overemphasize the transcendental nature of Spirit, thus condemning earth, nature, body, and woman to an inferior status. Prior to that, the matriarchal religions tended to emphasize the immanent nature of Spirit alone, and the resultant pantheistic worldview equated the finite and created Earth with the infinite and uncreated Spirit. You are free to identify with a finite and limited Earth; you are not free to call it the infinite and unlimited.

Both matriarchal and patriarchal religions, both of these lopsided views of Spirit, have had rather horrible historical consequences, from brutal and large-scale human sacrifice for the fertility of the earth Goddess to wholesale war for God the Father. But in the very midst of these outward distortions, the perennial philosophy (the esoteric or inner core of the wisdom religions) has always avoided any of those dualities—Heaven or Earth, masculine or feminine, infinite or finite, ascetic or celebratory—and centered instead on their union or integration ("nondualism"). And indeed, this union of Heaven and Earth, masculine and feminine, infinite and finite, ascending and descending, wisdom and compassion, was made explicit in the "tantric" teachings of the various wisdom traditions, from Neoplatonism in the West to Vajrayana in the East. And it is this nondual core of the wisdom traditions to which the term "perennial philosophy" most applies.

The point, then, is that if we are to try to think of Spirit in mental terms (which necessarily involves some difficulties), then at least we should remember this transcendent/immanent paradox. Paradox is simply the way nonduality looks to the mental level. Spirit itself is not paradoxical; strictly speaking, it is not characterizable at all.

This applies doubly to hierarchy (holarchy). We have said that when transcendental Spirit manifests itself, it does so in stages or levels—the Great Holarchy of Being. But I'm not saying Spirit or reality itself is hierarchical. Absolute Spirit or reality is not hierarchical. It is not qualifiable at all in mental terms (lower-holon terms)—it is *shunyata,* or *nirguna,* or apophatic—unqualifiable, without a trace of specific and limiting characteristics at all. But it manifests itself in steps, in layers, dimensions, sheaths, levels, or grades—whatever term one prefers—and that is holarchy. In Vedanta these are the *koshas,* the sheaths or layers covering Brahman; in Buddhism, these are the eight *vijñanas,* the eight levels of awareness, each of which is a stepped-down or more restricted version of its senior dimension; in Kabbalah these are the *sefirot,* and so on.

The whole point is that these are levels of the manifest world, of *maya.* When maya is not recognized as the play of the Divine, then it is nothing but illusion. Hierarchy is illusion. There are levels of illusion, not levels of reality. But according to the traditions, it is exactly (and only) by understanding the hierarchical nature of *samsara* that we can in fact climb out of it, a ladder discarded only after having served its extraordinary purpose.

Some postmodern critics have claimed that the very notion of the Great Chain, since it is hierarchical, is somehow oppressive; it is supposed to be based on unpleasant "ranking" instead of compassionate "linking." But this is a rather unsophisticated complaint. First, the antihierarchical and antiranking critics are themselves engaged in hierarchical judgments of ranking—namely, they claim their view is *better* than the alternatives. In other words, they themselves have a very strong ranking system; it's just hidden and inarticulate (and perfectly self-contradictory).

Second, the Great Chain was actually what Arthur Koestler called *a holarchy*: a series of concentric circles or nests, with each senior level transcending but including its juniors. This is a ranking, to be sure, but a ranking of increasing inclusiveness and embrace, with each senior level including more and more of the world and its inhabitants, so that the upper or spiritual reaches of the spectrum of consciousness are absolutely all-inclusive and all-embracing—a type of radical universal pluralism.

[THE EYE OF SPIRIT: 39–41, 43–45, 32–33]

Holons and Hierarchy

*H*iero- MEANS SACRED or holy, and -*arch* means governance or rule. Introduced by the great sixth-century Christian mystic Saint Dionysius the Areopagite, the "Hierarchies" referred to nine celestial orders, with Seraphim and Cherubim at the top and archangels and angels at the bottom. Among other things, these celestial orders represented higher knowledge and virtue and illuminations that were made more accessible in contemplative awareness. These orders were *ranked* because each successive order was more inclusive and more encompassing and in that sense "higher." "Hierarchy" thus meant, in the final analysis, "sacred governance," or "governing one's life by spiritual powers."

In the course of Catholic Church history, however, these celestial orders of contemplative awareness were translated into *political* orders of power, with the Hierarchies supposedly being represented in the pope, then archbishops, then bishops (and then priests and deacons). As Martineau put it in 1851, "a scheme of a hierarchy which might easily become a despotism." And already we can start to see how a normal developmental sequence of increasing wholes might pathologically degenerate into a system of oppression and repression.

As used in modern psychology, evolutionary theory, and systems theory, a hierarchy is simply a ranking of orders of events according to their *holistic capacity.* In any developmental sequence, what is whole at one stage becomes a part of a larger whole at the next stage. A letter is part of a whole word, which is part of a whole sentence, which is part of a whole paragraph, and so on. As How-ard Gardner explains it for biology, "Any change in an organism will affect all the parts; no aspect of a structure can be altered without affecting the entire structure; each whole contains parts and is itself part of a larger whole." Roman Jakobson for language: "The phoneme is a combination of distinctive features; it is composed of diverse primitive signaling units and can itself be in-corporated into larger units such as syllables and words. It is simul-taneously a whole composed of parts and is itself a part that is included in larger wholes."

Arthur Koestler coined the term *holon* to refer to that which, being a *whole* in one context, is simultaneously a *part* in another. With reference to the phrase "the bark of a dog," for example, the word *bark* is a whole with reference to its individual letters, but a part with reference to the phrase itself. And the whole (or the con-text) can determine the meaning and function of a part—the mean-ing of *bark* is different in the phrases "the bark of a dog" and "the bark of a tree." The whole, in other words, is more than the sum of its parts, and that whole can influence and determine, in many cases, the function of its parts (and that whole itself is, of course, simultaneously a part of some other whole).

Normal hierarchy, then, is simply an order of increasing holons, representing an increase in wholeness and integrative capacity-atoms to molecules to cells, for example. This is why hierarchy is indeed so central to systems theory, the theory of wholeness or holism ("wholism"). To be a part of a larger whole means that the whole supplies a principle (or some sort of glue) not found in the isolated parts alone, and this principle allows the parts to join, to link together, to have something in common, to be connected, in ways that they simply could not be on their own.

Hierarchy, then, converts heaps into wholes, disjointed frag-ments into networks of mutual interaction. When it is said that "the whole is greater than the sum of its parts," the "greater" means "hierarchy." It doesn't mean fascist domination; it means a higher (or deeper) commonality that joins isolated strands into an actual web, that joins molecules into a cell, or cells into an or-ganism.

This is why "hierarchy" and "wholeness" are often uttered in the same sentence, as when Gardner says that "a biological organism is viewed as a totality whose parts are integrated into a hierarchical whole." Or why, as soon as Jakobson explains language as "simultaneously a whole composed of parts and itself a part included in a larger whole," he concludes, "Hierarchy, then, is the fundamental structural principle." This is also why normal hierarchies are often drawn as a series of concentric circles or spheres or "nests within nests." As Goudge explains:

> The general scheme of levels is not to be envisaged as akin to a succession of geological strata or to a series of rungs in a ladder. Such images fail to do justice to the complex interrelations that exist in the real world. These interrelations are much more like the ones found in a nest of Chinese boxes or in a set of concentric spheres, for according to emergent evolutionists, a given level can contain other levels within it [i.e., holons].

Thus, the common charge that all hierarchies are "linear" completely misses the point. Stages of growth in any system can, of course, be written down in a "linear" order, just as we can write down: acorn, seedling, oak; but to accuse the oak of therefore being linear is silly. The stages of growth are not haphazard or random, but occur in some sort of pattern, but to call this pattern "linear" does not at all imply that the processes themselves are a rigidly one-way street; they are interdependent and complexly interactive. So we can use the metaphors of "levels" or "ladders" or "strata" only if we exercise a little imagination in understanding the complexity that is actually involved.

And finally, hierarchy is asymmetrical (or a "higher"-archy) because the process does not occur in the reverse. Acorns grow into oaks, but not vice versa. There are first letters, then words, then sentences, then paragraphs, but not vice versa. Atoms join into molecules, but not vice versa. And that "not vice versa" constitutes an unavoidable hierarchy or ranking or asymmetrical order of increasing wholeness.

All developmental and evolutionary sequences that we are aware of proceed by hierarchization, or by orders of increasing holism—molecules to cells to organs to organ systems to organisms to societies of organisms, for example. In cognitive development, we find awareness expanding from simple images, which represent only one thing or event, to symbols and concepts which represent whole groups or classes of things and events, to rules which organize and integrate numerous classes and groups into entire networks. In moral development (male or female), we find a reasoning that moves from the isolated subject to a group or tribe of related subjects, to an entire network of groups beyond any isolated element. And so on. . . .

These hierarchical networks necessarily unfold in a sequential or stagelike fashion, because you first have to have molecules, *then* cells, *then* organs, *then* complex organisms—they don't all burst on the scene simultaneously. In other words, growth occurs in *stages,* and stages, of course, are *ranked* in both a logical and chronological order. The *more holistic* patterns appear *later* in development because they have to await the emergence of the parts that they will then integrate or unify, just as whole sentences emerge only *after* whole words.

And some hierarchies do involve a type of control network. As Roger Sperry points out, the lower levels (which means, less holistic levels) can influence the upper (or more holistic) levels, through what he calls "upward causation." But just as important, he reminds us, the higher levels can exert a powerful influence or control on the lower levels—so-called "downward causation." For example, when you decide to move your arm, all the atoms and molecules and cells in your arm move with it—an instance of downward causation.

Now, *within* a given level of any hierarchical pattern, the elements of that level operate by *heterarchy.* That is, no one element seems to be especially more important or more dominant, and each contributes more or less equally to the health of the whole level (so-called "bootstrapping"). But a higher-order whole, of which this lower-order whole is a part, can exert an overriding influence on each of its components. Again, when you decide to move your arm, your mind—a higher-order holistic organization—exerts influence over all the cells in your arm, which are lower-order wholes, but *not vice versa*: a cell in your arm cannot decide to move the whole arm—the tail does not wag the dog.

And so systems theorists tend to say: *within* each level, heterarchy; *between* each level, hierarchy. In any developmental or growth sequence, as a more encompassing stage or holon emerges, it *includes* the capacities and patterns and functions of the previous stage (i.e., of the previous holons), and then adds its own unique (and more encompassing) capacities. In that sense, and that sense only, can the new and more encompassing holon be said to be "higher" or "deeper." ("Higher" and "deeper" both imply a vertical dimension of integration not found in a merely horizontal expansion.) Organisms *include* cells, which *include* molecules, which *include* atoms (but not vice versa).

Thus, whatever the important value of the previous stage, the new stage has that enfolded in its own makeup, plus something extra (more integrative capacity, for example), and that "something extra" means "extra *value*" *relative* to the previous (and less encompassing) stage. This crucial definition of a "higher stage" was first introduced in the West by Aristotle and in the East by Shankara and Lieh-tzu; it has been central to developmental studies ever since.

A quick example: in cognitive and moral development, in both the boy and the girl, the stage of preoperational or preconventional thought is concerned largely with the individual's own point of view ("narcissistic"). The next stage, the operational or conventional stage, still takes account of the individual's own point of view, but *adds* the capacity to take the *view of others* into account. Nothing fundamental is lost; rather, something new is added. And so in this sense it is properly said that this stage is higher or deeper, meaning more valuable and useful for a wider range of interactions. Conventional thought is *more valuable* than preconventional thought in establishing a balanced moral response (and postconventional is even more valuable, and so on).

The Essential Ken Wilber | 59

As Hegel first put it, and as developmentalists have echoed ever since, each stage is adequate and valuable, but each deeper or higher stage is more adequate and, in that sense only, more valuable (which always means more holistic, or capable of a wider response).

It is for all these reasons that Koestler, after noting that all hierarchies are composed of holons, or increasing orders of wholeness, pointed out that the correct word for "hierarchy" is actually *holarchy*.

Thus heterarchists, who claim that "heterarchy" and "holism" are the same thing (and that both are contrasted to the divisive and nasty "hierarchy"), have got it exactly backward: The only way to get a holism is via a holarchy. Heterarchy, in and by itself, is merely differentiation without integration, disjointed parts recognizing no common and deeper purpose or organization: heaps, not wholes.

[SEX, ECOLOGY, SPIRITUALITY: 17–21]

Reality Is Made of Holons

Reality as a whole is not composed of things or processes, but of holons. Composed, that is, of wholes that are simultaneously parts of other wholes, with no upward or downward limit. To say that holons are processes instead of things is in some ways true, but misses the essential point that processes themselves exist only within other processes. There are no things or processes, only holons.

Since reality is not composed of wholes, and since it has no parts—since there are only whole/parts—then this approach undercuts the traditional argument between atomism (all things are fundamentally isolated and individual wholes that interact only by chance) and wholism (all things are merely strands or parts of the larger web or whole). Both of those views are absolutely incorrect. There are no wholes, and there are no parts. There are only whole/parts.

This approach also undercuts the argument between the materialist and idealist camps. Reality isn't composed of quarks, or bootstrapping hadrons, or subatomic exchange; but neither is it composed of ideas, symbols, or thoughts. It is composed of holons.

There is an old joke about a King who goes to a Wiseperson and asks: How is it that the Earth doesn't fall down? The Wiseperson replies, "The Earth is resting on a lion." "On what, then, is the lion resting?" "The lion is resting on an elephant." "On what is the elephant resting?" "The elephant is resting on a turtle." "On what is the . . ." "You can stop right there, your Majesty. It's turtles all the way down."

Holons all the way down. "Subatomic particles are—in a certain sense which can only be defined rigorously in relativistic quantum mechanics—nested inside each other. The point is that a physical particle—a renormalized particle—involves (1) a bare particle and (2) a huge tangle of virtual particles, inextricably wound together in a recursive mess. Every real particle's existence therefore involves the existence of infinitely many other particles, contained in a virtual 'cloud' which surrounds it as it propagates. And each of the virtual particles in the cloud, of course, also drags along its own virtual cloud, bubbles within bubbles [holons within holons], and so on ad infinitum . . . [Hofstadter, *Gödel, Escher, Bach*].

But it's also turtles all the way up. Take mathematics, for example. The notorious "paradoxes" in set theory (Cantor's, Burali-Forti's, Russell's), which, among other things, led to Tarski's Theorem and Gödel's Incompleteness Theorem, placed mathematics in an *irreversible, ever-expanding, no-upper-limit universe*: "The totality of sets cannot be the terminus of a well-defined generating process, for if it were we could take all of what we had generated so far as a set and continue to generate still large universes. The totality of sets [mathematical holons] is an 'unconditioned or absolute totality which for just that reason cannot be adequately conceived by the human mind, since the object of a normal conception can always be incorporated in a more inclusive totality. Moreover, the sets are arranged in a transfinite hierarchy"—a holarchy that continues up*wardly forever, and must* continue upwardly forever ("transfinitely"), or mathematics comes to a screeching self-contradictory halt [P. Edwards, *The Encyclopedia of Philosophy*]. Even mathematics is set in time's arrow, and time's arrow is indefinitely—"transfinitely"—holarchical.

This is important for philosophy as well, and particularly for many of the "new age" paradigms that now trumpet "Wholism." "Transfinite" (turtles all the way up) means that the sum total of all the whole/parts in the universe is *not itself a Whole*, because the moment it comes to be (as a "whole"), that totality is merely a *part* of the very next moment's whole, which in turn is merely a part of the next . . . and so ad infinitum.

This means that there is no place where we can rest and say, "The universe's basic principle is Wholeness" (nor, of course, can we say, "The basic principle is Partness"). This prevents us from ever saying that the principle of the Whole rules the world, for it does not; any whole is a part, indefinitely.

Thus, holons within holons within holons means that the world is without foundation in either wholes or parts (and as for any sort of "absolute reality" in the spiritual sense, we will see that it is neither whole nor part, neither one nor many, but pure groundless Emptiness, or radically *nondual* Spirit).

This is important because it prevents a totalizing and dominating Wholeness. "Wholeness"—this is a very dangerous concept—dangerous for many reasons, not the least of which is that it is always available to be pushed into ideological ends. Whenever anybody talks of wholeness being the ultimate, then we must be very wary, because they are telling us that we are merely "parts" of their particular version of "wholeness," and so we should be subservient to their vision—we are merely strands in their wonderful web.

They like to engineer social utopias, these Wholists. This becomes all the more alarming when you simply ask them what is included in their "Wholeness," and you find out immediately that there are an enormous number of things that they do not include in their version of "the Whole." Ecofeminists do not include the patriarchy in their "whole"; most deep ecologists do not include meditative states in their "ultimate wholeness"; ecophilosophers in general do not like industrialization (or farming, for that matter), and so on. They may or may not be right; my point is that for people who claim to be embracing the Whole, these theorists reject an awful lot of existence.

In other words, since there is actually no such beast as the ultimate "Whole"—it simply does not exist anywhere—then those who peddle it have to give it content, not from reality, but solely from their own ideology. And then, since we are all defined as merely strands in their glorious web, a totalizing social agenda seems eminently reasonable. It is not beside the point that theorists as diverse as Habermas and Foucault have seen such totalizing agendas as the main modern enemy of the life-world.

I belabor this issue because it is extremely important to emphasize the indefiniteness of holarchy, its openness, its dizzyingly nesting nature—an actualization holarchy, not a dominator holarchy. And a dominator holarchy occurs precisely whenever any holon is established, not as a whole/part, but as the whole, period. "Ultimate Wholeness": this is the essence of dominator holarchies, pathological holarchies. "Pure wholeness": this is the totalizing lie.

For all these reasons, I usually refer to the sum total of events in the universe not as the "Whole" (which implies the ultimate priority of wholeness over partness) but as "the All" (which is the sum total of whole/parts). And this sum total is not itself a whole but a whole/part: as soon as you think "the All," your own thought has *added* yet another holon to the All (so that the first All is no longer *the* All but merely *part* of the new All), and so off we go indefinitely, never arriving at that which we symbolize as the "All," which is why it is *never* a whole, but an unending series of whole/parts (with the series itself a whole/part, and so on "transfinitely").

The Pythagoreans introduced the term *Kosmos,* which we usually translate as "cosmos." But the original meaning of Kosmos was the patterned nature or process of all domains of existence, from matter to math to theos, and not merely the physical universe, which is usually what both "cosmos" and "universe" mean today.

So I would like to reintroduce this term, *Kosmos.* The Kosmos contains the cosmos (or the physiosphere), the bios (or biosphere), nous (the noosphere), and theos (the theosphere or divine domain)—none of them being foundational (even spirit shades into Emptiness).

So we can say in short: The Kosmos is composed of holons, all the way up, all the way down.

[SEX, ECOLOGY, SPIRITUALITY: 35–38]

The Spectrum of Consciousness

The spectrum of consciousness is Wilber's model of human growth and development, integrating the systems developed by psychology with those of the contemplative traditions. The overall spectrum can be divided in various ways. In The Atman Project, *for example, Wilber gives seventeen basic levels, or structures, which make up the realms of matter, body, mind, soul, and spirit. These enduring structures of consciousness are what make up the Great Holarchy (Chain, Nest) of Being. For the purpose of summary, he has distilled the spectrum into seven or nine general ones—and further distilled into three major realms of development. The following two sections offer two different ways of subdividing the stages of development and simple explanations of them.*

See also "The Integral Approach," page 102, and "Completing the Great Chain," page 108. To study Wilber's model in depth, see the annotated bibliography at the end of the book.

SEVEN STAGES AND THREE REALMS

1. *Archaic*: This includes the material body, sensations, perceptions, and emotions. This is roughly equivalent to Jean Piaget's sensorimotor intelligence, Abraham Maslow's physiological needs, Jane Loevinger's autistic and symbiotic stages, the first and second *chakras, the annamayakosha* (physical food) and *pranamayakosha* (élan vital).

2. *Magic*: This includes simple images, symbols, and the first rudimentary concepts, or the first and lowest mental productions, which are "magical" in the sense that they display condensation, displacement, "omnipotence of thought," and so on. This is Freud's primary process, Arieti's paleologic, Piaget's preoperational thinking, the third *chakra*. It is *correlated* with Lawrence Kohlberg's preconventional morality, Loevinger's impulsive and self-protective stages, Maslow's safety needs, and so on.

3. *Mythic*: This stage is more advanced than magic, but not yet capable of clear rationality or hypothetico-deductive reasoning, a stage Jean Gebser explicitly termed "mythic." This is essentially Piaget's concrete operational thinking; the fourth *chakra*; the beginning of *manomayakosha* (Vedanta) and *manovijñana* (Mahayana). It is correlated with Loevinger's conformist and conscientious-conformist stages, Maslow's belongingness needs, Kohlberg's conventional stages, and so on.

4. *Rational*: This is Piaget's formal operational thinking, propositional or hypothetico-deductive reasoning; the fifth *chakra*; the culmination of *manomayakosha* and *manovijñana*. It is correlated with Loevinger's conscientious and individualistic stages, Kohlberg's post-conventional Morality, Maslow's self-esteem needs, and so on.

5. *Psychic*: Here I am including the centaur and the low-subtle as one general level. "Psychic" does not necessarily mean "paranormal," although some texts suggest that certain paranormal events may more likely occur here. Rather, it refers to "psyche" as a higher level of development than the mind per se (e.g., Aurobindo, Free John). Its cognitive structure has been called "vision logic," or integrative logic; the sixth *chakra*; the beginning of *manas* (Mahayana) and *vijñanamayakosha* (Vedanta). It is correlated with Loevinger's integrated and autonomous stages, Maslow's self-actualization needs, James Broughton's integrated stage, and so on.

6. *Subtle*: This is, basically, the archetypal level, the level of the "illumined mind" (Aurobindo); the culmination of *manas* and *vijñanamayakosha*; a truly transrational (not pre-rational and not anti-rational) structure; intuition in its highest and most sober sense;

not emotionalism or merely bodily felt meaning; home of Platonic forms; *bija-mantra, vasanas*; beginning of seventh chakra (and sub-chakras); start of Maslow's self-transcendence needs, and so on.

7. *Causal*: Or the unmanifest ground and suchness of all levels; the limit of growth and development; "Spirit" in the highest sense, not as a Big Person but as the "Ground of Being" (Tillich), "Eternal Substance" (Spinoza), "Geist" (Hegel); at and beyond the seventh *chakra; the anandamayakosha* (Vedanta), *alayavijñana* (Mahayana), *Keter* (Kabbalah), and so on.

Those seven general structure-stages of development can be further reduced to *three general realms*: the pre-rational (subconscious), the rational (self-conscious), and the transrational (superconscious). [See figure 1.]

[EYE TO EYE: 246–48]

NINE BASIC STRUCTURES, PATHOLOGIES, AND TREATMENTS

Growth and development occur through a series of stages or levels, from the least developed and least integrated to the most developed

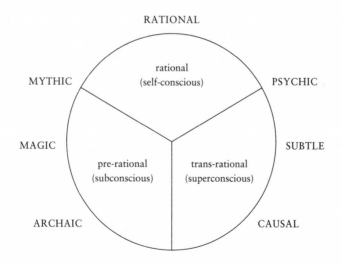

FIGURE 1. Three general realms and seven stages of development.
(Reprinted from *Eye to Eye*, p. 248.)

and most integrated. There are probably dozens of different levels and types of levels of growth; I have selected nine of the most important. These are listed in column one [of figure 2], "Basic Structures of Consciousness."

Now, as the self develops at each stage, things can go either relatively well or relatively poorly. If things go well, the self develops normally and moves on to the next stage in a relatively well-functioning way. But if things go persistently badly at a given stage, then various pathologies can develop, and the type of pathology, the type of neurosis, depends precisely on the stage or level at which the problem occurs [see figure 2].

In other words, at each stage or level of development, the self is faced with certain tasks. How it negotiates those tasks determines whether it winds up relatively healthy or relatively disturbed. First and foremost, at each stage of development, the self starts out identified with that stage, and it must accomplish the tasks appropriate to that stage, whether learning toilet training or learning language. But in order for development to continue, the self has to let go of that stage, or disidentify with it, in order to make room for the new and higher stage. In other words, it has to *differentiate* from the lower stage, identify with the higher stage, and then integrate the higher with the lower.

This task of differentiation and then integration is called a "fulcrum"—it just means a major turning point or a major step in development. So in column two [of figure 2], labeled "Corresponding Fulcrums," we have the nine major fulcrums or turning points that correspond to the nine major levels or stages of consciousness development. If anything goes persistently wrong at a given fulcrum, then you get a specific and characteristic pathology. These nine major pathologies are listed in column three, "Characteristic Pathologies." Here you find things like psychoses, neuroses, existential crises, and so on.

Finally, different treatment methods have evolved over the years to treat these various pathologies, and I've listed those treatments in column four, "Treatment Modalities," the treatments that I think have been demonstrated to be the best or more appropriate

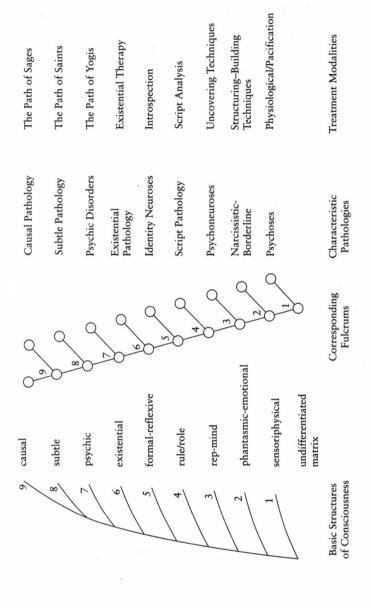

FIGURE 2. Correlation of structures, fulcrums, psychopathologies, and treatments. (Reprinted from *Grace and Grit*, p. 184.)

Basic Structures of Consciousness	Corresponding Fulcrums	Characteristic Pathologies	Treatment Modalities
causal	9	Causal Pathology	The Path of Sages
subtle	8	Subtle Pathology	The Path of Saints
psychic	7	Psychic Disorders	The Path of Yogis
existential	6	Existential Pathology	Existential Therapy
formal-reflexive	5	Identity Neuroses	Introspection
rule/role	4	Script Pathology	Script Analysis
rep-mind	3	Psychoneuroses	Uncovering Techniques
phantasmic-emotional	2	Narcissistic-Borderline	Structuring–Building Techniques
sensoriphysical	1	Psychoses	Physiological/Pacification
undifferentiated matrix			

for each particular problem. And this is exactly where the relation of psychotherapy and meditation comes in.

The basic structures are the fundamental building blocks of awareness, things like sensations, images, impulses, concepts, and so on. I have listed nine major basic structures, which are just an expanded version of what is known in the perennial philosophy as the Great Chain of Being: matter, body, mind, soul, and spirit. In ascending order, the nine levels are:

One, the sensoriphysical structures [the worldview of this level is called "archaic"]—these include the material components of the body plus sensation and perception. This is what Piaget called sensorimotor intelligence; what Aurobindo called the physical-sensory; what Vedanta calls the *annamayakosha,* and so on.

Two, the phantasmic-emotional [the beginning of the magical worldview]—this is the emotional-sexual level, the level of impulse, of libido, élan vital, bioenergy, *prana.* Plus the level of images, the first mental forms. Images—what Silvano Arieti calls the "phantasmic level"—start to emerge in the infant around seven months or so.

Three, the representational mind, or rep-mind for short [the transition from magical to mythic]—what Piaget called preoperational thinking. It consists of symbols, which emerge between the ages of two and four years, and then concepts, which emerge between the ages of four and seven.

What is the difference between images, symbols, and concepts? An image represents a thing by looking like that thing. It's fairly simple. The image of a tree, for example, looks more or less like a real tree. A symbol represents a thing but it doesn't look like that thing, which is a much harder and higher task. For example, the word "Fido" represents your dog, but it doesn't look like the real dog at all, and so it's harder to hold in mind. That's why words emerge only after images. Finally, a concept represents a *class* of things. The concept of "dog" means all possible dogs, not just Fido. A harder task still. A symbol denotes, a concept connotes. But symbols and concepts together we refer to as the preoperational or representational mind.

Level four, the rule/role mind [the mythic worldview], develops between the ages of seven and eleven or so, what Piaget called concrete operational thinking. The Buddhists call it the *manovijñana*, the mind concretely operating on sensory experience. I call it rule/role, because it is the first structure that can perform rule-dominated thinking, like multiplication or division, and it is the first structure that can take the role of other, or actually assume a perspective different from its own. It's a very important structure. Piaget calls it *concrete* operational because, although it can perform complex operations, it does so in a very concrete and literal way. This is the structure, for example, that thinks that myths are concretely true, literally true.

Level five, which I call formal-reflexive [the rational worldview], is the first structure that can not only think but think about thinking. It is thus highly introspective, and it is capable of hypothetical reasoning, or testing propositions against evidence. What Piaget called formal operational thinking. It typically emerges in adolescence, and is responsible for the burgeoning self-consciousness and wild idealism of that period. Aurobindo refers to this as the "reasoning mind"; Vedanta calls it the *manomayakosha*.

Level six is existential, or vision-logic, a logic which is not divisive but inclusive, integrating, networking, joining. What Aurobindo called the "higher mind"; in Buddhism, the *manas*. It is a very integrative structure. Particularly, it is capable of integrating the mind and body into a higher-order union, which I call the "centaur," symbolizing mind-body union (not identity).

Level seven is called psychic, which doesn't mean psychic capacities per se, although these might begin to develop here. But basically it just means the beginning stages of transpersonal, spiritual, or contemplative development. What Aurobindo called the "illumined mind."

Level eight is called the subtle, or the intermediate stage of spiritual development, the home of various luminous forms, divine forms or Deity forms, known as *yidam* in Buddhism and *ishtadeva* in Hinduism (not to be confused with the collective mythic forms of levels three and four). The home of a personal God, the home of the "real" transpersonal archetypes and supra-individual forms. Aurobindo's "intuitive mind"; *vijñanamaya-kosha* in Vedanta; in Buddhism, the *alayavijñana*.

Level nine is the causal, or the pure unmanifest source of all the other and lower levels. The home, not of a personal God, but of a formless Godhead or Abyss. Aurobindo's "overmind"; in Vedanta, the *anandamayakosha*, the bliss body.

Finally, the paper on which the entire diagram is drawn represents ultimate reality, or absolute Spirit, which is not a level among other levels but the Ground and Reality of all levels. Aurobindo's "supermind"; in Buddhism, the pure *alaya*; in Vedanta, *turiya*.

So level one is matter, level two is body, levels three, four, and five are mind. And level six is an integration of the mind and body, what I call the centaur, levels seven and eight are soul, and level nine plus the paper are Spirit.

[GRACE AND GRIT: 183–87]

The Centaur

The centaur is the great mythological being, half human and half animal body, that Wilber (among others, such as Hubert Benoit and Erik Erikson) has taken as a symbol of the harmonious integration of body and mind ("bodymind"), or biosphere and noosphere.

A S CONSCIOUSNESS BEGINS to transcend the verbal ego-mind, it can—more or less for the first time—integrate the ego-mind with all the lower levels. That is, because consciousness is no longer identified with any of these elements to the exclusion of any others, all of them can be integrated: the body, the persona, the shadow, the ego—all can be brought into a higher-order integration.

This stage is variously referred to as the "integration of all lower levels" (Sullivan, Grant, and Grant), "integrated" (Loevinger), "self-actualized" (Maslow), "autonomous" (Fromm, Riesman). According to Loevinger this stage represents an "integration of physiological and psychological," and Broughton's studies point to this stage as one wherein "mind and body are both experiences of an integrated self." This integrated self, wherein mind and body are harmoniously one, we call the "centaur." The centaur: the great mythological being with animal body and human mind existing in a perfect state of atonement.

On the whole, we can say that as one contacts and stabilizes on the centaur level, the elements of the gross personality—the body, the ego, the persona, the shadow, the lower *chakras*—tend to fall into harmony of themselves. For the individual is beginning to *transcend* them, and thus he ceases to compulsively manipulate and exploit them. All in all, this is the stage variously described as one of autonomy, of integration, of authenticity, or of self-actualization—the ideal of humanistic/existential therapies, the "highest" stage to which orthodox Western psychology aspires.

[THE ATMAN PROJECT: 53–54]

Healing the Bodymind Split

[T HERE ARE] ways to dissolve the boundary between the mind and body so as to discover again this unity of opposites lying asleep in the depths of our being. "This split cannot be overcome," says Alexander Lowen, "by a knowledge of the energetic processes in the body. Knowledge itself is a surface phenomenon and belongs to the realm of the ego. One has to feel the flow and sense the course of the excitation in the body. To do this, however, one must give up the rigidity of one's ego control so that the deep body sensations can reach the surface."

Simple as it sounds, that is the very difficulty almost every person faces as he tries to connect with his body. He won't really *feel* his legs, stomach, or shoulders, but, out of habit, he thinks about his legs, stomach, and shoulders. He pictures them to himself and thus avoids giving feeling-attention to them directly. This is, of course, one of the very mechanisms responsible for the dissociation of the body in the first place. Special attention should be given this tendency to conceptualize our feelings, and a special effort made to suspend, at least temporarily, this habitual translation of feeling-attention into thoughts and pictures.

One way to begin connecting with the body is by lying down on your back, outstretched, on a rug or mat. Simply close your eyes, breathe deeply but easily, and begin to explore your bodily feelings. Don't try to feel anything, don't force feelings, just let your attention flow through your body and note if any feeling, positive or negative, is present in the various parts of the body. Can you, for example, feel your legs? your stomach? your heart? eyes? genitals, buttocks, scalp, diaphragm, feet? Notice which parts of the body seem alive with feeling, full and strong and vital, and which parts seem dull, heavy, lifeless, dimmed, tight, or painful. Try this for at least three minutes, and notice how often your attention might leave the body and wander into daydreams. Does it strike you as odd that it might be very difficult to stay in your body for three minutes? If you're not in the body, where are you?

After this preliminary, we can move to the next step: still lying with your arms alongside and legs slightly parted, eyes closed, breathe very deeply but slowly, *drawing the inhalation from the throat to the abdomen,* eventually filling up your entire midsection. Imagine, if you like, that your entire chest and stomach is lined with a large balloon and that with each inhalation you are totally filling the balloon. The "balloon" should softly extend into the chest and bulge out fully and strongly in the abdomen. If you can't feel the gentle force of the expanded balloon in any of these areas, simply let the balloon fill out a little more, extending itself into that particular area. Then exhale slowly and smoothly, allowing the balloon to empty completely. Repeat this seven or eight times, maintaining the gentle but firm pressure inside the balloon so it bulges the abdomen and reaches the pelvic basin. Note especially which areas feel tight, tense, painful, or numb.

Can you feel that the entire ballooned area is one piece, or does it seem divided and segmented into chest, abdomen, and pelvic floor, each segment separated from the others by areas or bands of tightness, tension, or pain? In spite of these minor pains and discomforts, you might begin to notice that the feeling which extends throughout the balloon is one of subtle pleasure and joy. You are literally breathing in pleasure and radiating it throughout your bodymind. Upon exhalation, do not lose or exhaust the breath, but release it as pleasure to permeate the entire body. In this way, subtle pleasure flows through your bodymind and becomes fuller with each cycle. If you are not sure of this, complete another three or four total expansion breaths, yielding to the pleasure involved.

Perhaps you can start to understand why yogis call the breath a *vital force*—not in the philosophical sense, but in the feeling sense. Upon inhalation, you draw in a vital force from the throat to the abdomen, charging the body with energy and life. Upon exhalation, you release and radiate this force as subtle pleasure and joy throughout the bodymind itself.

You might continue the total expansion balloon breathing, inhaling vital force from the throat to the navel-abdomen (the *hara*), but start to feel the exhalation as a vital force radiating outward from the abdomen to all parts of the body. With each inhalation from the throat, charge the *hara* with vitality. Then, upon exhalation, see how far down and into each leg you can feel (or follow) the vital force or pleasure radiate-into the thighs? knees? feet? It eventually should go literally to the tips of the toes. Continue this for several breaths, and then try the same thing with the upper extremities. Can you feel the vitality being released into your arms? fingers? head, brain, and scalp? Then, upon exhalation, allow this subtle pleasure to pass through your body and *into the world at large*. Release your breath, through the body, to infinity.

Putting all these components together, we arrive at a complete breathing cycle: Upon inhalation, draw the breath from the throat to the *hara*, charging it with vital force. Upon exhalation, release this subtle pleasure *through* the entire bodymind to the world, to the cosmos, to infinity. Once this cycle becomes full, then start to allow all thinking to dissolve in the exhalation and pass to infinity. Do the same with all distressful feelings, with disease, with suffering, with pain. Allow feeling-attention to pass through all present conditions and then beyond them to infinity, moment to moment to moment.

We come now to the specifics of this type of exercise. More than likely you were able to feel vital pleasure and feeling-attention circulate easily throughout your bodymind. But in each aspect of this exercise you might also have felt some area of numbness, lack of feeling, or deadness on the one hand, or tightness, tension, rigidity, or pain on the other. You felt, in other words, blocks (miniboundaries) to the full flow of feeling-attention. Most people invariably feel tightness and tension in the neck, eyes, anus, diaphragm, shoulders, or lower back. Numbness is often found in the pelvic area, genitals, heart, lower abdomen, or the extremities. It's important to discover, as best you can, just where your own particular blocks exist. For the moment, *don't try to get rid of them*. At best, that won't work and at worst it will tighten them. Just find out where they seem to be, and mentally note the locations.

Once you have pinpointed these blocks, you can begin the process of dissolving them. But first we might consider just what these blocks and resistances mean—these areas or bands of tightness, pressure, and tension anchored throughout the body. We saw that on the ego level a person could resist and avoid an impulse or emotion by denying ownership of it. Through the mechanism of egoic projection, a person could prevent the awareness of a particular shadow tendency in himself. If he actually felt very hostile, but denied his own hostility, he would project it and thus feel that the world was attacking him. In other words, he would feel anxiety and fear, the result of projected hostility.

What is happening in the body when this hostility is projected? Mentally, a projection has occurred, but physically something else must happen simultaneously, since mind and body are not two. What happens in the body when you repress hostility? How, on the body level, do you suppress a strong emotion which seeks discharge in some activity?

If you get very hostile and angry, you might discharge this emotion in the activities of screaming, yelling, and striking out with the arms and fists. These muscular activities are the very essence of hostility itself. Thus, if you are to suppress hostility, you can only do so by physically suppressing these muscular discharge activities. You must, in other words, use your muscles to hold back these discharge activities. Rather, you must use *some* of your muscles to hold back the action of some of your other muscles. What results is a war of muscles. Half of your muscles struggle to discharge the hostility by striking out, while the other half strain to prevent just that. It's like stepping on the gas with one foot and the brake with the other. The conflict ends in stalemate, but a very tense one, with large amounts of energy expended with a net movement of zero.

In the case of suppressing hostility, you will probably clamp the muscles of your jaw, throat, neck, shoulders, and upper arms, for this is the only way you can physically "hold in" hostility. And hostility denied, as we have seen, usually floats into your awareness as fear. Thus, the next time you are in the grip of an irrational fear, notice that your whole shoulder area is pulled in and up, the sign that you are holding in hostility, and therefore feeling fear. But in your shoulders themselves you will *no longer feel* the tendency to reach out and attack; you will no longer feel hostility; you will only feel a strong tension, tightness, pressure. You have a block.

This is precisely the nature of the blocks which you located throughout your body during the breathing exercises. Every block, every tension or pressure in the body, is basically a *muscular* holding-in of some taboo impulse or feeling. That these blocks are muscular is an extremely important point. Note that these blocks and bands of tension are the result of two sets of muscles fighting each other (across a miniboundary), one set seeking to discharge the impulse, one set seeking to hold it in. And this is an active holding in, an "in-holding" or inhibiting. You literally crush yourself in certain areas instead of letting out the impulse associated with that area.

Thus, if you find a tension around the eyes, you might be in-holding a desire to cry. If you find a tension-ache in your temples, you may be clamping your jaws together unknowingly, perhaps trying to prevent screaming, yelling, or even laughing. A tension in the shoulder and neck indicates suppressed or in-held anger, rage, or hostility, while a tension in the diaphragm indicates that you chronically restrict and in-hold your breathing in an attempt to control the display of wayward emotions or feeling-attention in general. (During any act of self-control, most people will hold their breath.) Tension through the lower abdomen and pelvic floor usually means you have cut off all awareness of your sexuality, that you stiffen-up and in-hold that area to prevent the vital force of breath and energy from flowing through. Should this occur—for whatever reason—you will also shut off most feeling in your legs. And a tension, rigidity, or lack of strength in your legs usually indicates lack of rootedness, stability, groundedness, or balance in general.

Thus, as we have just seen, one of the best ways to understand the general meaning of a particular block is by noting where it occurs in the body. Particular body areas usually discharge particular emotions. You probably don't scream with your feet, cry with your knees, or have orgasms in your elbows. So if there is a block in a particular body area, we can assume the *corresponding* emotion is being suppressed and in-held.

Assuming you have now more or less located your major blocks to feeling, you can proceed to the really interesting endeavor: releasing and dissolving the blocks themselves. Although the basic procedure is simple to comprehend and easy enough to perform, the fruition of conscious results takes much hard work, effort, and patience. You probably have spent at least fifteen years building up a specific block, so you shouldn't be surprised if it doesn't vanish permanently after fifteen minutes of work. Like all boundaries, these take time to dissolve in conscious awareness.

If you have encountered these blocks before, you will realize that the most annoying aspect of them is that no matter how hard you try, you can't seem to relax them, at least not permanently. Through conscious effort you might succeed in going limp for a few minutes, but the tension (in your neck, back, chest, etc.) returns with a vengeance the moment you forget this "forced relaxation." Some blocks and tensions—perhaps most—refuse to relax at all. And yet the only remedy we habitually apply is the futile attempt to consciously relax these tensions (an approach, paradoxically enough, which itself demands a rather exhausting effort).

It seems, in other words, that these blocks *happen to us,* that they occur against our will, that they are wholly involuntary and uninvited. We seem to be their uncomfortable victims. Let us see, then, just what is involved in the persistence of these uninvited guests. The first thing to notice is that these blocks are all muscular, as we mentioned earlier. Each block is actually a contraction, a tightening, a locking of some muscle or group of muscles. Some group of *skeletal muscles*, that is, and *every skeletal muscle is under voluntary control.* The same voluntary muscles you use to move an arm, to chew, to walk, to jump, to make a fist, or to kick—just these same muscles are operating in every body block.

But that means that these blocks are not—indeed, they physically cannot be—involuntary. They do not happen to us. They are and must be something we are actively doing to ourselves. In short, we have deliberately, intentionally, and voluntarily created these blocks, since they consist solely of voluntary muscles.

Yet, curiously enough, we *don't know* that we are creating them. We are tightening these muscles, and although we know that they are tight and tense, we do not know that we are actively tensing them. Once this type of block occurs, we can't relax these muscles, simply because we don't know we are contracting them in the first place. It then appears that these blocks happen all by themselves (just like all other unconscious processes), and we seem helpless victims crushed by forces "beyond" our control.

This whole situation is almost exactly as if I were pinching myself but didn't know it. It is as if I intentionally pinched myself, but then forgot it was I who was doing the pinching. I feel the pain of the pinching, but cannot figure out why it won't stop. Just so, all of these muscular tensions anchored in my body are deep-seated forms of self-pinching. So the important question is not, "How can I stop or relax these blocks?" but rather, "How can I see that I am actively producing them?" If you are pinching yourself but don't know it, to ask somebody else to stop the pain does no good. To ask how to stop pinching yourself implies that *you aren't* doing it yourself. On the other hand, as soon as you see that you are actively pinching yourself, then, and only then, do you spontaneously stop. You don't go around asking how to stop pinching yourself, any more than you ask how to raise your hand. They are both voluntary actions.

The crux, therefore, is getting the direct feel of how I actively tense these muscles, and therefore the one thing I *don't* do is try to relax them. Rather, I must, as always, play my opposites. I must do what I would have never thought of doing before: I must actively and consciously attempt to *increase* the particular tension. By deliberately increasing the tension, I am making my self-pinching activity conscious instead of unconscious. In short, I start to remember how I have been pinching myself. I see how I have literally been attacking myself. That understanding felt through-and-through releases energy from the way of muscles, energy which I can then direct outward toward the environment instead of inward on myself. Instead of squeezing and attacking myself, I can "attack" a job, a book, a good meal, and thus learn afresh the correct meaning of the word aggression: "to move toward."

But there is a second and equally important aspect of dissolving these blocks. We have just seen that the first is to deliberately increase the pressure or tension by further tightening the muscles involved. In this way we do consciously what we have heretofore been doing unconsciously. But remember that these tension blocks were serving a most significant function—they were initially introduced to choke off feelings and impulses that at one time seemed dangerous, taboo, or unacceptable. These blocks were, and still are, forms of *resistance* to particular emotions. Thus, if these blocks are to be permanently dissolved, you will have to open yourself to the emotions which lie buried beneath the muscular cramp. It should be emphasized that these "buried feelings" are not some sort of wildly insatiable and totally overpowering orgiastic demands, nor some form of demonically possessing and bestial urges to wipe out your father and mother and siblings. They are most often rather mild, although they might seem dramatic because you have muscularly in-held them so long. They usually involve a release of tears, a good scream or two, ability for uninhibited orgasm, a good old-fashioned temper tantrum, or a temporary but enraged attack upon pillows set up for that purpose. Even if some fairly strong negative emotion surges up—some full-blown rage—it need not cause great alarm, for it does not constitute a major portion of your personality. In a live theatre play, when a minor two-line character walks on stage for the first time, all eyes in the audience turn to this minor player, even though he is an insignificant part of the total cast. Likewise, when some negative emotion first walks onto the stage of your awareness, you might become temporarily transfixed with it, even though it too is but a fragment of the total cast of your emotions. Much better to have it up front than rambling around backstage.

In any case, this emotional release, this upsurge of some type of in-held emotion, will usually happen of itself as you begin to consciously take responsibility for increasing the tightening of the muscles in the various blocks of the body. As you deliberately begin to contract the muscles involved, you tend to remember what it is you are contracting your muscles against. For example, if you see a friend about to cry, and you say, "Whatever you do, fight it!" he will probably burst into tears. At that moment he is deliberately trying to in-hold something natural to the organism, and he knows that he is trying to block it, so the emotion cannot easily go underground. In the same way, as you deliberately take charge of your blocks while trying to increase them, the inhibited emotion may start to surface and exhibit itself.

The entire procedure for this type of body awareness experiment might run as follows: After locating a specific block—let's say a tenseness in the jaw, throat, and temples—you give it your full awareness, feeling out just where the tension is and what muscles seem to be involved. Then, slowly but deliberately begin to increase that tension and pressure; in this case, by tightening your throat muscles and clamping your teeth together. While you are experimenting with increasing the muscular pressure, remind yourself that you are not just clamping muscles, *you are actively trying to hold something in.* You can even repeat to yourself (out loud if your jaws aren't involved), "No! I won't! I'm resisting!" so that you truly feel that part of yourself that is doing the pinching, that is trying to in-hold some feeling. Then you can slowly release the muscles and at the same time open yourself totally to whatever feeling would like to surface. In this case, it might be a desire to cry, or to bite out, or to vomit, or to laugh, or to scream. Or it might only be a pleasurable glow where the block used to be. To allow a genuine release of blocked emotions requires time, effort, openness, and some honest work. If you have a typically persistent block, daily "workouts" of fifteen minutes or so for upwards of a month will almost certainly be necessary for significant results. The block is released when feeling-attention can flow through that area in a full and perfectly unobstructed fashion on its way to infinity.

[NO BOUNDARY: 109–16]

Experiential, Intellectual, and Spiritual

Experience IS BASICALLY just another word for awareness. If I experience my body, it means I am aware of my body. You can indeed be aware of your body, but you can also be aware of your mind—you can right now notice all the thoughts and ideas and images floating in front of the mind's inward eye. You can, in other words, *experience your mind*, be aware of your mind. And it's very important to be able to experience your mind directly, cleanly, intensely, because only by bringing awareness to the mind can you begin to transcend the mind and be free of its limitations. When that begins to happen, usually in meditation or contemplation, you can have even higher experiences, spiritual experiences, mystical experiences—*satori, kensho, samadhi,* and so on. You can, we might say, be aware of spirit, experience spirit, although in a more nondual manner.

So you can *experience* body, mind, and spirit. All of those are *experiential.* So perhaps you can begin to understand why it is a catastrophe to reduce experiential to *just the body,* to just bodily sensations, feelings, emotions, impulses, and so on. This is a reductionistic nightmare. It denies the higher experiential realities of the mind and spirit: it denies intellect and buddhi, higher mental vision and imagery and dreams, higher rational discrimination and perspectivism and moral depth, higher formless awareness and deeply contemplative states—all are denied or reduced.

The body, you see, is basically narcissistic and egocentric. Bodily feelings are just about *your* body, period. The body's sensations cannot take the role of other—that's a mental capacity, and therefore the body's sensory awareness cannot enter into care and compassion and ethical discourse and I-thou spirituality—all of those demand a cognitive, mental, intellectual awareness. To the extent you "stay in your body" and are "anti-intellectual," then you stay in the orbit of your own narcissism.

So that's the first mistake in the "experiential versus intellectual" prejudice—all of the experiential modes are reduced to bodily experiences only, which is the essence of egocentrism. The second mistake is to then reduce spiritual experiences to bodily experiences. The idea is that if you stay focused in your body, focused in your feelings, that these are the direct door to spirituality, because they transcend the mind. But bodily sensations and feelings and emotions are not transrational, they are prerational. By staying only in the body, you are not beyond the mind, you are beneath it. You are not transcending, you are regressing—becoming more and more narcissistic and egocentric, focusing on your own feelings. And this, if anything, prevents actual spiritual experiences, because genuine spirituality is "bodymind dropped"—that is, you cease identifying exclusively with both the feelings of the body and the thoughts of the mind, and this you cannot do if you merely "stay in the body."

So anytime you hear somebody tell you to be "experiential" instead of "intellectual," you can almost be certain they are making these two simple but crucial mistakes. They are taking all the experiences of body, mind, and spirit and claiming that only the body experiences are real—the lowest of the experiential domains!—and then they are reducing spiritual experiences to bodily experiences. Both are a nightmare, really.

But the thing is, it's even worse than that. Although we can accurately speak of bodily, mental, and spiritual experiences, the fact is, the highest spiritual states are not even *experiences*. Experiences, by their very nature, are temporary; they come, stay a bit, and pass. But the Witness is not an experience: it is aware of experiences, but it is not itself experiential in the least. The Witness is the vast openness and freedom in which experiences arise, and through which experiences pass. But the Witness itself never enters the stream of time—it is aware of time—and thus it never enters the stream of experiences.

So even here, to say that Spirit is experiential (versus intellectual) is still to completely distort Spirit, because Spirit is not a passing experience but the formless Witness of all experience. To remain stuck in experiences is to remain ignorant of Spirit.

[ONE TASTE: August 12]

The Pre/Trans Fallacy

EVER SINCE I began writing on the distinctions between prerational (or prepersonal) states of awareness and transrational (or transpersonal) states—what I called the pre/trans fallacy—I have become more convinced than ever that this understanding is absolutely crucial for grasping the nature of higher (or deeper) or truly spiritual states of consciousness.

The essence of the pre/trans fallacy is itself fairly simple: since both prerational states and transrational states are, in their own ways, nonrational, they appear similar or even identical to the untutored eye. And once pre and trans are confused, then one of two fallacies occurs:

In the first, all higher and transrational states are *reduced* to lower and prerational states. Genuine mystical or contemplative experiences, for example, are seen as a regression or throwback to infantile states of narcissism, oceanic adualism, indissociation, and even primitive autism. This is, for example, precisely the route taken by Freud in *The Future of an Illusion*.

In these reductionistic accounts, rationality is the great and final omega point of individual and collective development, the high-water mark of all evolution. No deeper or wider or higher context is thought to exist. Thus, life is to be lived either rationally, or neurotically (Freud's concept of neurosis is basically anything that derails the emergence of rational perception—true enough as far as it goes, which is just not all that far). Since no higher context is thought to be real, or to actually exist, then whenever any genuinely transrational occasion occurs, it is immediately explained as a *regression* to prerational structures (since they are the only nonrational structures allowed, and thus the only ones to accept an explanatory hypothesis). The superconscious is reduced to the subconscious, the transpersonal is collapsed to the prepersonal, the emergence of the higher is reinterpreted as an irruption from the lower. All breathe a sigh of relief, and the rational worldspace is not fundamentally shaken (by "the black tide of the mud of occultism!" as Freud so quaintly explained it to Jung).

On the other hand, if one is sympathetic with higher or mystical states, but one still *confuses* pre and trans, then one will *elevate* all prerational states to some sort of transrational glory (the infantile primary narcissism, for example, is seen as an unconscious slumbering in the *mystico unio*). Jung and his followers, of course, often take this route, and are forced to read a deeply transpersonal and spiritual status into states that are merely indissociated and undifferentiated and actually lacking any sort of integration at all.

In the elevationist position, the transpersonal and transrational mystical union is seen as the ultimate omega point, and since egoic-rationality does indeed tend to deny this higher state, then egoic-rationality is pictured as the *low point* of human possibilities, as a debasement, as the cause of sin and separation and alienation. When rationality is seen as the anti-omega point, so to speak, as the great Anti-Christ, then anything nonrational gets swept up and indiscriminately glorified as a direct route to the Divine, and consequently the most infantile and regressive and prerational occasions get a field promotion on the spot: *anything* to get rid of that nasty and skeptical rationality. "I believe *because* it is absurd" (Tertullian)—there is the battle cry of the elevationist (a strand that runs deeply through Romanticism of any sort).

Freud was a reductionist, Jung an elevationist—the two sides of the pre/trans fallacy. And the point is that they are *both* half right and half wrong. A good deal of neurosis is indeed a fixation/regression to prerational states, states that are not to be glorified. On the other hand, mystical states do indeed exist, beyond (not beneath) rationality, and those states are not to be reduced.

For most of the recent modern era, and certainly since Freud (and Marx and Ludwig Feuerbach), the reductionist stance toward spirituality has prevailed—all spiritual experiences, no matter how highly developed they might in fact be, were simply interpreted as regressions to primitive and infantile modes of thought. However, as if in overreaction to all that, we are now, and have been since the sixties, in the throes of various forms of elevationism (exemplified by, but by no means confined to, the New Age movement). All sorts of endeavors, of no matter what origin or of what authenticity, are simply elevated to transrational and spiritual glory, and the only qualification for this wonderful promotion is that *the endeavor be nonrational. Anything* rational is wrong; *anything* nonrational is spiritual.

Spirit is indeed nonrational; but it is trans, not pre. It transcends but includes reason; it does not regress and exclude it. Reason, like any particular stage of evolution, has its own (and often devastating) limitations, repressions, and distortions. But the inherent problems of one level are solved (or "defused") only at the next level of development; they are not solved by regressing to a previous level where the problem can be merely ignored. And so it is with the wonders and the terrors of reason: it brings enormous new capacities and new solutions, while introducing its own specific problems, problems solved only by a transcendence to the higher and transrational realms.

Many of the elevationist movements, alas, are not beyond logic but beneath it. They think they are, and they announce themselves to be, climbing the Mountain of Truth; whereas, it seems to me, they have merely slipped and fallen and are sliding rapidly down it, and the exhilarating rush of skidding uncontrollably down evolution's slope they call "following your bliss." As the earth comes rushing up at them at terminal velocity, they are bold enough to offer this collision course with ground zero as a new paradigm for the coming world transformation, and they feel oh-so-sorry for those who watch their coming crash with the same fascination as one watches a twenty-car pileup on the highway, and they sadly nod as we decline to join in that particular adventure. True spiritual bliss, in infinite measure, lies up that hill, not down it.

[SEX, ECOLOGY, SPIRITUALITY: 206–208]

Rationality Means Perspective

SOME PEOPLE, I BELIEVE, are put off by the notion that rationality (and vision-logic) might somehow be a *necessary* prerequisite for higher or transpersonal development. And these folks especially do not trust this notion when it comes from egghead theorists. Does the transpersonal really "integrate" the rational, and if so, what about nontechnological cultures that do not seem to access rationality? Do we deny them Spirituality?

Developmental psychologists (such as Kegan) and philosophers (such as Habermas) tend to use "rational" in a very broad and general fashion, which sometimes confuses people. The simple capacity to *take the perspective of another person,* for example, is a rational capacity. You must be able mentally to step out of your own perspective, cognitively picture the way the world looks to the other person, and then place yourself in the other's shoes, as it were—all extremely complicated cognitive capacities, and all referred to as "rational" in the very general sense.

Thus, as I explain in *Sex, Ecology, Spirituality,* rational in this broad sense means, among other things, the capacity for perspectivism, for sustained introspection, and for imagining "as-if" and "what-if" possibilities. Rationality, to put it simply, is the sustained capacity for cognitive *pluralism and perspectivism.*

Some theorists have claimed that "rationality" (as used by Piaget or Habermas) might actually be, in effect, Eurocentric, and that its "lack" in other cultures might reflect Western biases. But, as Alexander et al. point out, several researchers "have convincingly argued that formal operational capacities are evident within non-technological societies when tasks appropriate to the culture are employed." Rationality doesn't mean you have to be Aristotle; it means you can take perspectives. This is why Habermas maintains that even in foraging societies, formal operations were available to a significant number of men and women. You are operating within reason when you operate within perspective. You don't have to be doing calculus.

Likewise, vision-logic does not mean that you have to be Hegel or Whitehead. Rationality means perspective; vision-logic means integrating or coordinating different perspectives. Even in the earliest foraging tribes, it is quite likely that a chieftain would have to take multiple perspectives in order to coordinate them: vision-logic. The Western forms of reason and vision-logic are just that: Western forms; but the deep capacities themselves are not.

But you can't coordinate perspectives if you can't take perspective in the first place; and you can't take perspective if you can't take the role of other. And there, once again, is the limited but crucial role of the stage conception.

And yes, I most definitely believe that *postconventional* spirituality depends upon the capacity to coordinate different perspectives. I do not believe, for example, that the bodhisattva vow can operate fully without it—without, that is, vision-logic. I believe it is the gateway through which stable *psychic, subtle, causal, and nondual stages* of spirituality must pass, and upon which they rest. Indeed, by definition, the bodhisattva vow rests upon vision-logic, and if you have ever vowed to liberate all perspectives, you have operated with vision-logic.

Nevertheless, you certainly can have spiritual development without perspectival reason and without integral-aperspectival vision-logic, for the simple reason that the spiritual line is a quasi-independent line of development. The spiritual line goes right down to the archaic, sensorimotor level, where one's religion—one's ultimate concern—is food. And the spiritual line will continue through the early prerational realms (magical, egocentric). With the capacity to take the role of other, the spiritual line will begin to expand its ultimate concern from the self to the group and its beliefs (mythic-membership). From there it will learn to take a more universal perspective (mythic-rational, rational), where its ultimate concern will begin to include the welfare of a global humanity, regardless of race, gender, creed. That awareness will flower into a global vision-logic, with its concern for *all sentient beings as such,* and that will be the platform of the transpersonal spiritual stages themselves, which take as their foundation the liberation of the consciousness of all sentient beings without exception.

Thus, you can have all sorts of spirituality without "integrating reason." But you cannot have a global spirituality, a bodhisattvic spirituality, a post-postconventional spirituality, an authentically transpersonal spirituality, unless the perspectives of all sentient beings are taken into account and fully honored. Unless, that is, you integrate the deep capacities of reason and vision-logic, and then proceed from there.

Anybody can say they are being "spiritual"—and they are, because everybody has some type and level of concern. Let us therefore see their actual conception, in thought and action, and see how many perspectives it is in fact concerned with, and how many perspectives it actually takes into account, and how many perspectives it attempts to integrate, and thus let us see how deep and how wide runs that bodhisattva vow to refuse rest until all perspectives whatsoever are liberated into their own primordial nature.

[THE EYE OF SPIRIT: 229–31]

The Romantic View

THE CRUCIAL ERROR of the Romantic view is fairly easy to understand. Take childhood, for example. The Romantic view is that the infant starts out in a state of *unconscious Heaven*. That is, because the infant self isn't yet differentiated from the environment around it (or from the mother), the infant self is actually one with the dynamic Ground of Being—but in an unconscious (or "un-self-conscious") fashion. Thus, unconscious Heaven—blissful, wonderful, mystical, the paradisiacal state out of which it will soon fall, and to which it will always long to return.

And indeed, the Romantic view continues, sometime in the first few years of life, the self differentiates from the environment, the union with the dynamic Ground is lost, subject and object are separated, and the self moves from unconscious Heaven into conscious Hell—the world of egoic alienation, repression, terror, tragedy.

But, the happy account continues, the self can make a type of U-turn in development, sweep back to the prior infantile, union state, re-unite with the great Ground of Being, only now in a fully conscious and self-actualized way, and thus find conscious Heaven.

And so the overall Romantic view: one starts out in unconscious Heaven, an unconscious union with the Divine; one then *loses* this unconscious union, and thus plunges into conscious Hell; one can then regain the Divine union, but now in a higher and conscious fashion.

The only problem with that view is that the first step—the loss of the unconscious union with the Divine—is an absolute impossi-

The Essential Ken Wilber | 95

bility. All things are one with the Divine Ground—it is, after all, the Ground of all being! To lose oneness with that Ground is to cease to exist.

Follow it closely: there are only two general stances you can have in relation to the Divine Ground: since all things are one with Ground, you can either be aware of that oneness, or you can be unaware of that oneness. That is, you can be conscious or unconscious of your union with the Divine Ground: those are the only two choices you have.

And since the Romantic view is that you start out, as an infant, in an unconscious union with Ground, you *cannot then lose that union*! You have *already* lost consciousness of the union; you cannot then further lose the union itself or you would cease to be! So if you start out unconscious of your union, it can't get any worse, ontologically speaking. That is already the pits of alienation. You are already living in Hell, so to speak; you are already immersed in *samsara*, only you don't realize it; you haven't the awareness to recognize this. And so that is more the actual state of the infantile self: unconscious Hell.

What does start to happen, however, is that you begin to wake up to the alienated world in and around you. You go from unconscious Hell to *conscious* Hell, and being conscious of Hell, of *samsara*, of lacerating existence, is what makes growing up—and being an adult—such a nightmare of misery and alienation. The infant self is relatively peaceful, not because it is living in Heaven, but because it isn't aware enough to register the flames of Hell all around it. The infant is most definitely immersed in *samsara*, it just doesn't know it, it isn't aware enough to realize it, and enlightenment is certainly not a return to this infantile state! Or a "mature version" of this state! Neither the infant self nor my dog writhes in guilt and angst and agony, but enlightenment does not consist in recapturing dog-consciousness (or a mature form of dog-consciousness!).

As the infant self grows in awareness and consciousness, it slowly becomes aware of the intrinsic pain of existence, the torment inherent in *samsara*, the mechanism of madness coiled inherently in the manifest world: it begins to suffer. It is introduced to the first Noble Truth, a jolting initiation into the world of perception, whose sole mathematics is the torture-inducing fire of unquenched and unquenchable desire. This is not a desire-ridden world that was lacking in the infant's previous "wonderful" immersion state, but simply a world that dominated that state unconsciously, a world which the self now slowly, painfully, tragically becomes aware of.

And so, as the self grows in awareness, it moves from unconscious Hell to conscious Hell, and there it may spend its entire life, seeking above all else the numbing consolations that will blunt its raw and ragged feelings, blur its etchings of despair. Its life becomes a map of morphine, and folding itself into the anesthetic glow of all its compensations, it might even manage to convince itself, at least for an endearing blush of rose-tinted time, that the dualistic world is an altogether pretty thing.

But alternatively, the self might continue its growth and development into the genuinely spiritual domains: transcending the separate-self sense, it uncoils in the very Divine. The union with the Divine—a union or oneness that had been present but unconscious since the start—now flares forth in consciousness in a brilliant burst of illumination and a shock of the unspeakably ordinary: it realizes its Supreme Identity with Spirit itself, announced, perhaps, in nothing more than the cool breeze of a bright spring day, this outrageously obvious affair.

And thus the actual course of human ontogeny: from unconscious Hell to conscious Hell to conscious Heaven. *At no point does the self lose its union with the Ground,* or it would utterly cease to be! In other words, the Romantic agenda is right about the second and third steps (the conscious Hell and the conscious Heaven), but utterly confused about the infantile state itself, which is not unconscious Heaven but unconscious Hell.

Thus, the infantile state is not unconscious transpersonal, it is basically prepersonal. It is not transrational, it is prerational. It is not transverbal, it is preverbal. It is not trans-egoic, it is pre-egoic. And the course of human development—and *evolution at large*—is from subconscious to self-conscious to superconscious; from pre-personal to personal to transpersonal; from under-mental to mental to over-mental; from pre-temporal to temporal to trans-temporal, by any other name: eternal.

The Romantics had simply confused pre with trans, and thus elevated the pre states to the glory of the trans (just as the reductionists would dismiss the trans states by claiming they were regression to pre states). These two confusions—the elevationist and the reductionist—are the two main forms of the pre/trans fallacy, which was first outlined and identified in [*The Atman Project*]. And the crucial point was that development is not regression in service of ego, but evolution in transcendence of ego.

Now, there is indeed a *falling away* from Godhead, from Spirit, from the primordial Ground, and this is the truth the Romantics are trying to get at, before they slip into their pre/trans fallacies. This falling away is called *involution*, the movement whereby all things fall away from a consciousness of their union with the Divine, and thus imagine themselves to be separate and isolated monads, alienated and alienating. And once involution has occurred—and Spirit becomes unconsciously involved in the lower and lowest forms of its own manifestation—*then evolution* can occur: Spirit unfolds, from the Big Bang to matter to sensation to perception to impulse to image to symbol to concept to reason to psychic to subtle to causal occasions, on the way to its own shocking self-recognition, Spirit's own self-realization and self-resurrection. And in each of those stages—from matter to body to mind to soul to spirit—evolution becomes more and more conscious, more and more aware, more and more realized, more and more awake—with all the joys and all the terrors inherently involved in that dialectic of awakening.

At each stage of this process of Spirit's return to itself, we—you and I—nonetheless remember, perhaps vaguely, perhaps intensely, that we were once consciously one with the very Divine itself. It is there, this memory trace, in the back of our awareness, pulling and pushing us to realize, to awaken, to remember who and what we always already are.

In fact, all things, we might surmise, intuit to one degree or another that their very Ground is Spirit itself. All things are driven, urged, pushed, and pulled to manifest this realization. And yet, prior to that divine awakening, all things seek Spirit in a way that actually prevents the realization: or else we would be realized right now! We seek Spirit in ways that prevent it.

We seek for Spirit in the world of time; but Spirit is timeless, and cannot there be found. We seek for Spirit in the world of space; but Spirit is spaceless, and cannot there be found. We seek for Spirit in this or that object, shiny and alluring and full of fame or fortune; but Spirit is not an object, and it cannot be seen or grasped in the world of commodities and commotion.

In other words, we are seeking for Spirit in ways that prevent its realization, and force us to settle for substitute gratifications, which propel us through, and lock us into, the wretched world of time and terror, space and death, sin and separation, loneliness and consolation.

And that is the Atman project.

The Atman project: the attempt to find Spirit in ways that prevent it and force substitute gratifications. The entire structure of the manifest universe is driven by the Atman project, a project that continues until we—until you and I—awaken to the Spirit whose substitutes we seek in the world of space and time and grasping and despair. The nightmare of history is the nightmare of the Atman project, the fruitless search in time for that which is finally timeless, a search that inherently generates terror and torment, a self ravaged by repression, paralyzed by guilt, beset with the frost and fever of wretched alienation—a torture that is only undone in the radiant Heart when the great search itself uncoils, when the self-contraction relaxes its attempt to find God, real or substitute: the movement in time is undone by the great Unborn, the great Uncreate, the great Emptiness in the Heart of the Kosmos itself.

And so, try to remember: remember the great event when you breathed out and created this entire Kosmos; remember the great emptying when you threw yourself out as the entire World, just to see what would happen. Remember the forms and forces through which you have traveled thus far: from galaxies to planets, to verdant plants reaching upward for the sun, to animals stalking day and night, restless with their weary search, through primal men and women, yearning for the light, to the very person now holding this book: remember who and what you have been, what you have done, what you have seen, who you actually are in all those guises, the masks of the God and the Goddess, the masks of your own Original Face.

Let the great search wind down; let the self-contraction uncoil in the immediateness of present awareness; let the entire Kosmos rush into your being, since you are its very Ground; and then you will remember that the Atman project never occurred, and you have never moved, and it is all exactly as it should be, when the robin sings on a glorious morning, and raindrops beat on the temple roof.

[THE EYE OF SPIRIT, 52–56]

The Big Three: I, We, and It

WHEN YOU ARE ultimately *truthful* with yourself, you will eventually realize and *confess* that "I am Buddha," I am Spirit. Anything short of that is a lie, the lie of the ego, the lie of the separate-self sense, the contraction in the face of infinity. The deepest recesses of your consciousness directly intersect Spirit itself, in the supreme identity. "Not I, but Christ liveth in me"—which is to say, the ultimate I *is* Christ. This is not a state you are bringing into existence for the first time, but simply a timeless state that you are recognizing and confessing—you are being ultimately *truthful* when you state, "I am Buddha," the ultimate Beauty.

And the ultimate cultural fit or justness is, "We are all members of the Community of Spirit." All *sentient beings*—all holons, in fact—contain Buddha-nature—contain depth, consciousness, intrinsic value, Spirit—and thus we are all members of the council of all beings, the mystical church, the ultimate We. Which is ultimate ethics, the ultimate Good.

And the ultimate objective truth is that all beings are perfect manifestations of Spirit or Emptiness—we are all manifestations of the ultimate It, or Dharma. Which is the ultimate Truth.

The ultimate I, the ultimate We, and the ultimate It—Buddha, Sangha, Dharma.

[A BRIEF HISTORY OF EVERYTHING:132]

The Essential Ken Wilber | 101

The Integral Approach

THERE ARE MANY WAYS to explain "integral" or "holistic." The most common is that it is an approach that attempts to include and integrate matter, body, mind, soul, and spirit—attempts, that is, to include the entire Great Nest of Being. Thus, physics deals with matter, biology deals with the living body, psychology deals with the mind, theology deals with the soul, and mysticism deals with the direct experience of spirit—so an integral approach to reality would include physics, biology, psychology, theology, and mysticism (to give just a few examples).

Although that is a good start at defining "integral," what I have tried to do in my writings is make that scheme a little more sophisticated by pointing out that each of those *levels* actually has at least four important aspects or dimensions. Each level can be looked at from the inside and from the outside in both individual and collective forms.

For example, your consciousness can be looked at from the inside—the subjective side, your own awareness right now—which is experienced in the first person as an "I" (all the images, impulses, concepts, and desires floating through your mind right now). You can also study consciousness in an objective, empirical, scientific fashion, in the third person as an "it" (for example, the brain contains acetylcholine, dopamine, serotonin, etc., all described in objective it-language). And both of those exist not just in singular but in plural forms—not just an "I" or an "it," but a "we." This collective form also has an inside and outside: the cultural values shared from within, and the exterior concrete social forms seen from without.

So each level in the Great Chain actually has an *inside* and an *outside* in both individual and *collective* forms—and that gives us the four dimensions (or "four quadrants") of each level of existence. [See figure 3.]

Because both of the Right-Hand quadrants are objective its, they can be counted as one, so I often simplify the four dimensions to

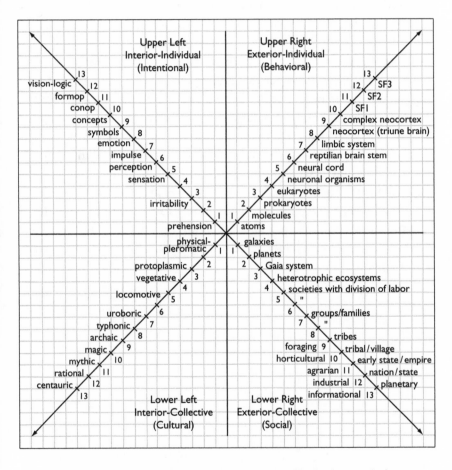

FIGURE 3. The four quadrants. (*SF* in the Upper Right stands for "structure-function"; see *Sex, Ecology, Spirituality*.)
(Reprinted from *A Brief History of Everything*, p. 74.)

just three: I, we, and it; or first-person, second-person, and third-person.

There's an easy way to remember these three basic dimensions. *Beauty* is in the eye of the beholder, the "I" of the beholder. The *Good* refers to moral and ethical actions that occur between you and me—that is, "we." *Truth* usually refers to objective empirical facts, or "its." So the three basic dimensions of "I," "we," and "it" also refer to the Beautiful, the Good, and the True. Or again, art, morals, and science. So a truly integral view would not talk just about matter, body, mind, soul, and spirit—because *each* of those levels has a dimension of art, of morals, and of science, and we need explicitly to include all of them. So, for example, we have the art of the matter/body realm (naturalism, realism), the art of the mental realm (surrealistic, conceptual, abstract), the art of the soul and spirit realm (contemplative, transformative). Likewise, we have morals that spring from the sensory realm (hedonism), from the mental realm (reciprocity, fairness, justice), and from the spiritual realm (universal love and compassion). And so on.

So putting these three *dimensions* (I, we, and it; or art, morals, and science; or Beauty, Goodness, and Truth) together with the major levels of existence (matter, body, mind, soul, and spirit) would give us a much more genuinely integral or holistic approach to reality.

[ONE TASTE: March 15]

Integral Practice

THERE ARE MANY WAYS to talk about integral practice. "Integral yoga" was a term first used by Aurobindo (and his student Chaudhuri), where it specifically meant a practice that unites both the ascending and descending currents in the human being—not just a transformation of consciousness, but of the body as well.

Mike Murphy's *Future of the Body* is an excellent compendium of an integral view, as is Tony Schwartz's *What Really Matters*. I outline my own integral approach in *The Eye of Spirit*. Murphy and Leonard's *The Life We Are Given* is a practical guide to one type of integral practice, and is highly recommended.

But anybody can put together their own integral practice. The idea is to simultaneously exercise all the major capacities and dimensions of the human bodymind—physical, emotional, mental, social, cultural, spiritual. To give several examples, going around the quadrants, we have the following capacities and levels, with some representative practices from each:

UPPER RIGHT QUADRANT
(INDIVIDUAL, OBJECTIVE, BEHAVIORAL)

Physical
DIET: Pritikin, Ornish, The Zone, Bob Arnot; vitamins, hormones
STRUCTURAL: weight lifting, aerobics, hiking, Rolfing, etc.

Neurological
> PHARMACOLOGICAL: various medications, where appropriate
> BRAIN/MIND MACHINES: to help induce theta and delta states of awareness

UPPER LEFT QUADRANT
(INDIVIDUAL, SUBJECTIVE, INTENTIONAL)

Emotional
> BREATH: t'ai chi, yoga, bioenergetics, circulation of *prana* or feeling-energy, qi gong
> SEX: tantric sexual communion, self-transcending whole-bodied sexuality

Mental
> THERAPY: psychotherapy, shadow work, cognitive therapy
> VISION: adopting a conscious philosophy of life, visualization, affirmation

Spiritual
> PSYCHIC (shaman/yogi): shamanic, nature mysticism, beginning tantric
> SUBTLE (saint): deity yoga, *yidam*, prayer, advanced tantric
> CAUSAL (sage): *vipassana*, self-inquiry, bare attention, witnessing
> NONDUAL (*siddha*): Dzogchen, Mahamudra, Shaivism, Zen, etc.

LOWER RIGHT QUADRANT
(SOCIAL, INTEROBJECTIVE)

Systems: exercising responsibilities to Gaia, nature, biosphere, and geopolitical infrastructures at all levels

Institutional: exercising educational, political, and civic responsibilities to town, state, nation, world

LOWER LEFT QUADRANT
(CULTURAL, INTERSUBJECTIVE)

Relationships: with family, friends, sentient beings in general; making relationships part of one's growth, decentering the self

Community Service: volunteer work, homeless shelters, hospice, etc.

Morals: engaging the intersubjective world of the Good, practicing compassion in relation to all sentient beings

The general idea of integral practice is clear enough: *Pick a basic practice from each category,* or from as many categories as pragmatically possible, and *practice them concurrently.* The more categories that are engaged, the more effective they all become (because they are all intimately related as aspects of one's own being). Practice them diligently, and coordinate your integral efforts to unfold the various potentials of the bodymind—until the bodymind itself unfolds in Emptiness, and the entire journey is a misty memory from a trip that never even occurred.

[ONE TASTE: June 18]

Completing the Great Chain

A S SCHOLARS FROM Ananda Coomaraswamy to Huston Smith have pointed out, the core of the perennial philosophy is the Great Chain of Being, the Great Nest of Being. But it is now apparent that there are at least four crippling inadequacies to the Great Chain as it was traditionally conceived, and in order to bring it into the modern and postmodern world, these shortcomings need to be carefully addressed.

The Great Chain is traditionally given as matter, body, mind, soul, and spirit. Many traditions subdivide this considerably. For example, the soul is often divided into *psychic* and *subtle* levels, and spirit into causal and nondual. An expanded Great Nest would therefore include: matter, body, mind, soul (psychic and subtle), and spirit (causal and nondual).

That is fine. But those levels are supposed to include *all of reality.* Yet, as stated, they mostly apply to just the Upper Left quadrant (the spectrum of interior consciousness)—and that's the first inadequacy. Thus, as I have often tried to point out, each of the *vertical levels* of the Great Chain needs to be differentiated into four *horizontal dimensions* (the four quadrants). So in addition to the subjective spectrum of consciousness, we need to add objective correlates (the Upper Right quadrant), intersubjective cultural backgrounds (Lower Left quadrant), and collective social systems (Lower Right). [See "The Integral Approach," page 106.] Otherwise the Great Chain cannot withstand the blistering critiques that modernity has (correctly) leveled at it.

The second inadequacy is that the level of mind needs to be subdivided in the light of its *early development*. Here the contributions of Western psychology shine forth most brightly. To put it in a nutshell, the mind itself has at least four major stages of growth: *magic* (2–5 years), *mythic* (6–11 years), *rational* (11 onward), and integral-aperspectival or *vision-logic* (adulthood, if then).

If we put all this evidence together, drawing on the East and West alike, then a more complete Great Nest of Being would include these ten spheres, each of which enfolds its predecessor(s) in a development that is envelopment:

1. *Sensorimotor*: the physical body, the material level, the physiosphere.
2. *Emotional-sexual*: biological drives, sensations, perceptions, feelings; life energy, élan vital, libido, prana, bioenergy.
3. *Magic*: the early form of the mind, where subject and object are poorly differentiated. It is marked by egocentrism, artificialism, animism, anthropocentrism, and word magic. Because inside and outside are poorly differentiated, objects are imbued with human egoic intentions. Likewise, the narcissistic ego believes that it can directly and magically alter the world (Saturday-morning children's cartoons are largely of the magical structure: superheroes can move mountains just by a glance; they can fly, melt steel, zap enemies, and otherwise push the world around by sheer magical power). In short, because subject and object are not yet clearly differentiated, the magical ego treats the world as an extension of itself and imbues that world with its own egoic traits. Narcissism and egocentrism rule.
4. *Mythic*: an intermediate level of mind, where magical power is shifted from the ego to a host of mythic gods and goddesses; if the ego cannot miraculously alter the world at will, the gods and goddesses can. In magic, the ego *itself* always has the power to perform miracles; in myth, the power to perform miracles is always possessed by a great Other. Thus magic uses rituals to display its own miraculous power; myth uses *prayer*

in an attempt to get the god or goddess to perform the miracle for it. Myth is the beginning realization that the ego cannot itself magically push the world around; it is thus a lessening of narcissism, a diminution of egocentrism.

5. *Rational*: a highly differentiated function of the mind that dispenses with concrete-literal myths and attempts instead to secure its needs through evidence and understanding. Neither egocentric magic nor mythic god figures are going to miraculously intervene in the course of Kosmic events just to satisfy your egoic desires. If you want something from the Kosmos, you are going to have to understand it on its own terms, following its own evidence; the birth of a truly scientific attitude, another lessening of narcissism.

6. *Vision-logic*: the highest function of the gross-realm mind; a synthesizing, unifying mode of cognition. Vision-logic does not achieve unity by ignoring differences but embracing them—it is integral-aperspectival—it finds universal pluralism and unity-in-diversity.

7. *Psychic*: the beginning of the transpersonal, supraindividual, or spiritual realms. This level is often marked by an intense mystical union with the entire gross realm—the sensorimotor realm of nature, Gaia, the World Soul. The home of *nature mysticism*.

8. *Subtle*: the subtle realm proper is the home, not of gross-realm mythological god and goddess figures focused on your ego, but of directly cognized, vividly intense, and ontologically real Forms of your own highest Self. The home of genuine *Deity mysticism*.

9. *Causal*: the causal realm per se, the formless unmanifest, pure Emptiness. The root of the Witness. The home of *formless mysticism*.

10. *Nondual*: this is both the highest Goal of all stages, and the ever-present Ground of all stages. The union of Form and Emptiness. The home of integral or *nondual mysticism*.

That is a much more complete Great Chain or spectrum of consciousness (a more complete Upper Left quadrant). Each of those levels actually has four dimensions or four quadrants, but even on its own, this more complete Great Nest allows us to do several important things at once:

- Stop elevating magic and mythic to psychic and subtle. This elevation of magical narcissism to transcendental glory is the single defining characteristic of the New-Age movement.
- Stop confusing mythological stories with transpersonal awareness. This elevation of myth to subtle illumination is rampant in countercultural spirituality.
- Stop confusing holistic vision-logic with magical indissociation. This elevation of magical cognition, which confuses whole and part, to the status of vision-logic, which *integrates* whole and part, is one of the defining moves of the "new paradigm" and "web-of-life" ideologies, and is epidemic in eco-primitivism (or the belief that foraging tribes integrated self, culture, and nature, whereas—as theorists from Lenski to Habermas to Gebser have pointed out—they actually failed to differentiate them in the first place; this was predifferentiated fusion, not transdifferentiated integration).
- Stop confusing the biosphere, bioenergy, and *prana* (level 2) with the World Soul (level 7). This elevation of ecology to World Soul is the single defining characteristic of ecopsychology, ecofeminism, and deep ecology. (It often joins the previous confusion—that of magic with vision-logic—to recommend a catastrophic regression to foraging cultures.)

Those examples could be multiplied almost indefinitely. Suffice it to say that, with a more complete Great Holarchy of Being, we can in fact spot the *regressive* nature of many of those movements. Thus the great wisdom traditions, when complemented by Western psychology, help us to move forward, not backward.

Here is the problem, correctable by Western developmental psychology: In the traditional depiction of the Great Chain (e.g., matter, body, mind, psychic, subtle, causal, and nondual), the "mind" level almost always meant the logical or rational faculty, and anything nonrational had to be placed on the higher, transrational levels because the early, *prerational* stages of development were poorly understood. These early, prerational levels can be grasped only by an intense investigation of infant and child development, an almost exclusive contribution of the modern West.

In other words, the traditional Great Chain (in Christianity, Hinduism, Buddhism, Sufism, Taoism, paganism, Goddess-worship, etc.) was—*and most definitely still is*—open to massive pre/trans fallacies, because it has no way to differentiate magic and mythic from psychic and subtle—they *all* get placed in the transpersonal/transrational domain. This catastrophic confusion was responsible, in no small measure, for the Western Enlightenment's complete and total rejection of spirituality, since so much of it (and the Great Chain) was obviously full of dogmatic magic and myth. The West correctly tossed the baby of prerationality, but it also, unfortunately, tossed a ton of transrational bathwater with it.

(Today's countercultural spiritual seekers repeat the same mistake of the traditional Great Chain theorists, upon whom they often rely: Every time some sort of magic or mythic story is found, it is instantly assumed that this *must* be representing transrational realities, whereas just as often it is a prerational regression. And if you don't agree with their prerational magic and myth, you are accused of being anti-spiritual.)

The third inadequacy: Because the traditional Great Chain theorists had a poor understanding of the early, infantile, prerational stages of human development, they likewise failed to grasp the types of *psychopathologies* that often stem from complications at these early stages. In particular, psychosis can often stem from problems at stages 1–2; borderline and narcissistic disorders, stages 2–3; and psychoneurosis, stages 3–4.

Western depth psychology has amassed compelling evidence for these pathologies and their genesis, and the Great Chain needs desperately to be supplemented with these findings. As it is, every time the Great Chain theorists were confronted with a case of mental madness—and lacking an understanding of the prerational stages—they were forced to assume it was a wild descent of transrational God, whereas it was, more often than not, a frightening resurgence of prerational id. These poor deranged people were rarely God-intoxicated; they were borderline basket cases. Treating them as God-realized is right up there with sacred cows—and did *nothing* to assuage modernity's suspicion that *all* of spirituality is a nut case. If babbling idiots and cows are enlightened, why listen to Eckhart and Teresa and Rumi, either?

The fourth inadequacy in the traditional Great Chain is its lack of understanding of evolution, an understanding that is also a rather exclusive contribution of the modern West. The funny thing—as many theorists have pointed out—is that if you tilt the Great Chain on its side and let it unfold in time (instead of being statically given all at once, as traditionally thought), you have the outlines of evolution itself. Plotinus temporalized = evolution.

In other words, evolution to date—starting with the Big Bang—has unfolded approximately three-fifths of the Great Chain, in precisely the order predicted: insentient matter to living bodies to conceptual mind (or physiosphere to biosphere to noosphere). All that is required is to see that the Great Chain does not exist fully given and statically unchanging, but rather evolves or develops over great periods of time, with each of the higher levels emerging through (not from) the lower. And the fact is, despite the bluff of Western biologists, nobody really understands how higher stages emerge in evolution—*unless* we assume it is via Eros, or Spirit-in-action.

Evolution in the cultural domain is, of course, a politically incorrect topic, which almost certainly means it is true. Numerous theorists have come around to this view. In recent times, cultural evolution has been championed, in various ways, by Jürgen Habermas, Gerald Heard, Michael Murphy, W. G. Runciman, Sisirkumar Ghose, Alastair Taylor, Gerhard Lenski, Jean Houston, Duane Elgin, Jay Earley, Daniel Dennett, Robert Bellah, Erwin Laszlo, Kishore Gandhi, and Jean Gebser, to name a few. The pioneering work of Jean Gebser is probably paradigmatic for the lot: he sees cultural worldviews evolving—to use his words—from *archaic* to *mythic* to *mental* to *integral*. Sound familiar?

The point is that, once the Great Chain is plugged into an evolutionary and developmental view, it can happily coexist with much of the God of the modern West, namely, evolution. Moreover, it raises the stunning possibility: if evolution has thus far unfolded the first three-fifths of the Great Chain, isn't it likely that it will continue in the coming years and unfold the higher two-fifths? If that is so, God lies down the road, not up it; Spirit is found by going forward, not backward; the Garden of Eden lies in our future, not our past.

Those are four inadequacies of the Great Chain of Being that have thoroughly prevented it from being accepted by modernity (doesn't cover the four quadrants; doesn't take early, prerational development into account, and thus is open to massive pre/trans fallacies; doesn't understand early pathologies; doesn't grasp evolution). Conversely, repairing those deficiencies can—and, I believe, will—make the Great Holarchy fully compatible with modern research, evidence, and information, thus uniting the best of ancient wisdom with the brightest of modern knowledge.

[ONE TASTE: June 5]

Waves and Streams in Consciousness

I N *The Eye of Spirit*, I divide my work into four main phases: wilber-1 was Romantic; wilber-2 was basically the Great Chain understood in developmental terms (a model first presented in *The Atman Project*); wilber-3 goes considerably further and suggests that there are numerous different developmental lines that progress relatively independently through the various levels of the Great Chain (a model first presented in *Transformations of Consciousness* and fleshed out in *The Eye of Spirit*); and wilber-4 sets those levels and lines in the context of the four quadrants (the psychological component of wilber-3 and wilber-4 are essentially the same, so I often refer to my latest psychological model as wilber-3, with the understanding that it is simply the Upper Left quadrant of wilber-4). . . .

Here is a simple way to picture wilber-3, which involves the integration of the *levels* of the Great Chain with various developmental *lines* moving through those levels (or streams through those waves). Let's use a simple version of the Great Chain, with only four levels (body, mind, soul, and spirit); let's use only five lines (there are almost two dozen); and let's make spirituality *both* the highest development in each line *and* a separate line of its own, to cover both common definitions (see figure 4).

Since "hierarchy" upsets many people, let's also draw that hierarchy in the way that it is actually defined, namely, as a holarchy (see figure 5). This is the identical concept, but some people are more comfortable with nice feminine circles (I prefer them myself,

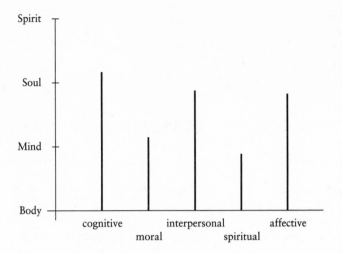

FIGURE 4. The Integral Psychograph

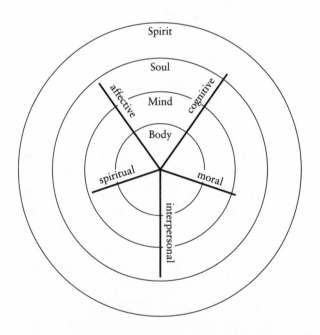

FIGURE 5. The Integral Psychograph as a Holarchy

because they so clearly show the "transcend and include" nature of the Great Nest of Being).

The point of both of those diagrams—what I call an "integral psychograph"—is that you can track the different developmental lines (or streams) as they move through the various levels (or waves) of the Great Nest. You can be at a higher, transpersonal, or "spiritual" level in several lines, and at a lower, personal, or "psychological" level in others, so that both spiritual and psychological development overlap—and the separate spiritual line(s) can be relatively high or low as well.

All of these streams and waves are navigated by the self (or the self system), which has to balance all of them and find some sort of harmony in the midst of this mélange. Moreover, something can go wrong in any stream at any of its waves (or stages), and therefore we can map various types of pathologies wherever they occur in the psychograph—different types of pathologies occur at different levels or waves in each of the lines.

Even though we can say, based on massive evidence (clinical, phenomenological, and contemplative), that many of these developmental streams proceed through the waves in a stage-like fashion, nonetheless *overall* self development does *not* proceed in a specific, stagelike manner, simply because the self is an amalgam of all the various lines, and the possible number of permutations and combinations of those is virtually infinite. Overall individual growth, in other words, follows no set sequence whatsoever.

Finally, as suggested in the nested diagram (figure 5), because each senior dimension transcends but includes (or nests) the junior dimension, to be at a higher wave does not mean the lower waves are left behind. This is not (and never has been) based on a ladder, but on the model of: atoms, molecules, cells, and organisms, with each senior level enfolding or enveloping the junior—as Plotinus put it, a development that is envelopment. So even at a higher level, "lower" work is still occurring simultaneously—cells still have molecules, Buddhas still have to eat.

That's wilber-3 in a nutshell. While I'm on that topic, I'll give one last example of why I believe that this type of wilber-3 model is an improvement on the traditional Great Chain model (or wilber-2), which contains the various *levels* of Being but does not fully understand how and why different *lines* develop through those levels. Huston Smith, we have seen, accurately summarizes the traditional Great Chain as body, mind, soul, and spirit (correlative with realms he calls terrestrial, intermediate, celestial, and infinite). That model is fine as far as it goes, but the trouble is, it starts to fall apart under further scrutiny, and it completely collapses under the avalanche of modern psychological research.

To begin with, the traditional Great Chain tends to confuse the levels of Being and the types of self-sense associated with each level. For example, mind is a *level* of the Great Chain, but the ego is the *self* generated when consciousness *identifies* with that level (i.e., identifies with mind). The subtle is a level of the Great Chain, the soul is the self generated when consciousness identifies with the subtle. The causal/spirit is a level in the Great Chain, the True Self is the "self" associated with that level, and so on. So the sequence of levels in the Great Chain should be body, mind, subtle, and causal/spirit, with the correlative self stages of bodyego, ego, soul, and Self—to use the very simplified version. Although I often use the traditional terminology (body, mind, soul, spirit), I always have in mind the difference between the actual levels (body, mind, subtle, causal) and the self at those levels (bodyego, ego, soul, Self).

Here is where some of these distinctions start to pay off (and the usefulness of the move from wilber-2 to wilber-3 becomes more obvious). The traditions generally maintain that men and women have two major personality systems, as it were: the *frontal* and the *deeper psychic*. The traditional Great Chain theorists (and wilber-2) would simply say that the frontal is the self associated with the body and mind, and the deeper psychic is associated with the soul, which would indeed be a type of ladder arrangement. But the frontal and the deeper psychic seem much more flexible than that; they seem to be, not different levels, but separate lines, of development, so that their development occurs alongside of, not on top of, each other. We can graph this as shown in figure 6 (for which I have reverted to a more accurate six levels).

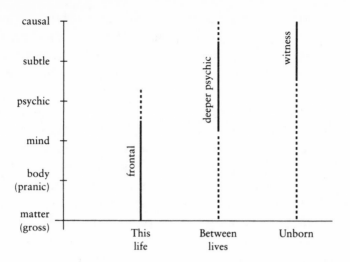

FIGURE 6. The Development of the Frontal (or Ego), the Deeper Psychic (or Soul), and the Witness (or Self).

The frontal being is the *gross-oriented personality*—in the wildest sense, what we mean by "ego," or the personality that is oriented outwardly to the sensorimotor world. The frontal being begins its developmental line or stream with material conception, continues through the emotional-sexual or pranic stages, into the mental stages, and fades out at the psychic. *Frontal development* represents the evolution of the self (or self-identity) through the lower-to-intermediate waves of the Great Nest of Being.

According to the traditions, while the frontal personality is that which develops in this life, the deeper psychic is that which develops between lives. It is, in the very widest sense, what we mean by the word "soul." At any rate, the deeper psychic is said to be present sometime from conception to midterm; in fact, some research suggests that prenatal, perinatal, and neonatal memories do in fact exist, and since these cannot be carried by the frontal personality and the gross brain (since they have not developed), the traditions would maintain that these memories are being carried by the deeper psychic being and are later lost as frontal development gets under way and submerges the early psychic being. Likewise, past-life memories, if they are genuine, would be carried by the deeper psychic. Nonetheless, it is not necessary to believe in either prenatal memory or past lives in order to acknowledge the deeper psychic self, which is *primarily* defined by its access to higher consciousness, not by its access to past lives.

Although the deeper psychic is present from birth (or mid-prenatal), it plays a modest role until the *necessary* frontal development finishes its task of orienting (and adapting) consciousness to the gross realm. As the frontal personality begins to fade, the deeper psychic being comes increasingly to the fore. Just as the frontal personality orients consciousness to the gross realm, the deeper psychic orients consciousness to the subtle realm. And, as we saw, the self associated with the subtle realm is the "soul," which is why "deeper psychic" and "soul" are generally synonymous. But the deeper psychic, even though its roots are in the subtle realm per se, nonetheless has a development that reaches down to some of the earliest stages, culminates in the subtle, and disappears at the causal.

Already we can begin to see the advantage of making the frontal and the deeper psychic not discrete levels but overlapping lines; not different waves but often parallel streams. We can go one step further and note that there is a last major "personality," that of the Self, associated with the causal, but also, like the others, having developments that reach down into earlier stages. In other words, we can usefully treat the Self as a separate line or stream of development, even though its basic orientation is the causal.

The Self, or the transpersonal Witness, is not—like the ego or the soul—a "personality," since it has no specific characteristics whatsoever (it is pure Emptiness and the great Unborn), except for the fact that it is an Emptiness still separate from Form, a Witness still divorced from that which is witnessed. As such, the Self or Witness is the seat of attention, the root of the separate—self sense, and the home of the last and subtlest duality, namely, that between the Seer and the seen. It is both the highest Self, and the final barrier, to nondual One Taste.

Nonetheless, the power of Witnessing is the power of liberation from all lower domains, and the Witness itself is present, even if latently, at all previous stages. Each developmental stage "transcends and includes" its predecessor, and the "transcend" aspect, in every case, is the power of the higher to be aware of the lower (the soul is aware of the mind, which is aware of the body, which is aware of matter). And in each case, the "is aware of" is simply the power of the Witness shining through at that stage.

Although the Witness is present as the power of transcendental growth at every stage, it comes to its own fruition in the causal realm. *As the ego orients consciousness to the gross, and the soul orients consciousness to the subtle, the Self orients consciousness to the causal.* While all of them have their root dispositions in specific realms or waves of the Great Nest, they also have their own lines or streams of development, so they often overlap each other, as indicated in figure 6. And this is what I think so many mediation teachers and transpersonal therapists see in themselves and their clients, namely, that *ego and soul and Spirit can in many ways coexist and develop together,* because they are relatively separate streams flowing through the waves in the Great Nest of Being. And there can be, on occasion, rather uneven development in between these streams.

We all know fairly enlightened teachers (alive to the Unborn) who nonetheless still have "big egos," in the sense of strong, forceful, powerful personalities. But the presence of the ego is not a problem; it all depends upon whether the person is *also* alive to higher and deeper dimensions. As Hubert Benoit said, it is not the identification with the ego that is the problem, but the exclusive nature of that identification. When our self-identity expands beyond the ego, into the deeper psychic, then even into the Unborn and One Taste, the ego is simply taken up and subsumed in a grander identity. But the ego itself remains as the functional self in the gross realm, and it might even appropriately be intensified and made more powerful, simply because it is now plugged into the entire Kosmos. Many of the great enlightened teachers had a big ego, a big deeper psychic, and a very big Self, all at once, simply because these are the three functional vehicles of the gross, subtle, and causal domains, and all three vehicles were appropriately intensified in the great awakened ones.

Now—and this is what tends to confuse people—although the various developmental lines often overlap each other, and in no specific sequence, the *individual lines or streams themselves usually have their own invariant, universal, developmental sequence*—namely, to the extent that they unfold into consciousness, they must negotiate the levels or waves in the Great Nest, and in an order that is given by Nest itself. For example, we have substantial evidence that cognition, morals, affects, kinesthetic skills, and interpersonal capacity, to name a few, all develop through preconventional, conventional, and postconventional waves. In other words, the various streams seem to move through the levels in the Great Nest in a fashion that is determined by the universal Great Nest itself. Although all sorts of regressions and temporary leaps forward are possible, the empirical fact remains as Aurobindo said: individual streams obey the law of a successive unfolding (undulating through the waves of the Great Nest itself).

At the same time, I repeat: even though all developmental lines (including the frontal, the deeper psychic, and the capacity for witnessing) follow their own stages, the *overall* mixture of lines does not. The "overall self" is a juggling of some two dozen different developmental lines, and thus each individual's unfolding will thus be a radically unique affair.

[ONE TASTE: November 16]

Buddhism and the Stages of Development

I DO NOT THINK that Buddhism is the best way or the only way. And I would not especially call myself a Buddhist; I have too many affinities with Vedanta Hinduism and Christian mysticism, among many others. But one has to choose a particular path if one is to actually practice, and my path has been Buddhist. So I have ended up with Chesterton's quip: "All religions are the same, especially Buddhism."

Where I do think Buddhism excels is in its completeness. It has specific practices that address all of the higher stages of development—psychic, subtle, causal, and ultimate. And it has a graded system of practice that leads you, step by developmental step, through each of these stages, limited only by your own capacity for growth and transcendence....

Tibetan Buddhism divides the overall spiritual path into three broad stages (each with several substages): the Hinayana, the Mahayana, and the Vajrayana.

The Hinayana is the foundation practice, the basic and core practice found in all schools of Buddhism. Central to this stage is the practice of *vipassana*, or insight meditation. In *vipassana*, one simply sits in a comfortable position (lotus or half-lotus if possible, cross-legged if not), and one gives "bare attention" to whatever is arising, externally and internally, without judging it, condemning it, following after it, avoiding it, or desiring it. One simply wit-

nesses it, impartially, and then lets it go. The aim of this practice is
to see that the separate ego is not a real and substantial entity, but
just a series of fleeting and impermanent sensations like anything
else. When one realizes just how "empty" the ego is, one ceases
identifying with it, defending it, worrying about it, and this in turn
releases one from the chronic suffering and unhappiness that
comes from defending something that isn't there. As Wei Wu Wei
put it:

> Why are you unhappy?
> Because 99.9% of everything you think,
> And everything you do,
> Is for your self,
> And there isn't one.

. . . As profound as this practice is, it is still not complete, because there is still a subtle dualism contained in pure witnessing
awareness itself. There are many technical ways to explain this,
but the simplest is: the Hinayana level aims at enlightenment for
oneself but neglects the enlightenment of others. And doesn't that
show that there is some trace of ego left, getting yours and neglect-
ing others?

And so, where the Hinayana teachings stress individual enlightenment, the Mahayana teachings go one step further and also
stress the enlightenment of all beings. It is thus the path, first and
foremost, of compassion, and this is meant not just in a theoretical
sense; there are actual practices for developing compassion in your
own mind and heart.

Foremost among these practices is the one known as *tonglen*,
which means "taking and sending." After one has developed a
strong foundation practice in *vipassana*, one *moves* on to the practice of *tonglen*. This practice is so powerful and so transformative
it was kept largely secret until just recently in Tibet. The practice
is as follows:

In meditation, picture or visualize someone you know and love
who is going through much suffering—an illness, a loss, depres-

sion, pain, anxiety, fear. As you breathe in, imagine all of that person's suffering—in the form of dark, black, smokelike, tarlike, thick, and heavy clouds—entering your nostrils and traveling down into your heart. Hold that suffering in your heart. Then, on the out-breath, take all of your peace, freedom, health, goodness, and virtue, and send it out to the person in the form of healing, liberating light. Imagine they take it all in, and feel completely free, released, and happy. Do that for several breaths. Then imagine the town that person is in, and, on the in-breath, take in all of the suffering of that town, and send back all of your health and happiness to everyone in it. Then do that for the entire state, then the entire country, the entire planet, the universe. You are taking in all the suffering of beings everywhere and sending them back health and happiness and virtue.

When people are first introduced to this practice, their reactions are usually strong, visceral, and negative. Mine were. Take that black tar into me? Are you kidding? What if I actually get sick? This is insane, dangerous! When Kalu Rinpoche first gave these *tonglen* instructions [during a retreat], a woman stood up in the audience of about one hundred people and said what virtually everybody there was thinking:

"But what if I am doing this with someone who is really sick, and I start to get that sickness myself?"

Without hesitating Kalu said, "You should think, Oh good! It's working!"

That was the entire point. It caught all of us "selfless Buddhists" with our egos hanging out. We would practice to get our own enlightenment, to reduce our own suffering, but take on the suffering of others, even in imagination? No way.

Tonglen is designed exactly to cut that egoic self-concern, self-promotion, and self-defense. It exchanges self for other, and thus it profoundly undercuts the subject/object dualism. It asks us to undermine the self/other dualism at exactly the point we are most afraid: getting hurt ourselves. Not just talking about having compassion for others' suffering, but being willing to take it into our own heart and release them in exchange. This is true compassion, the path of the Mahayana. In a sense it is the Buddhist equivalent of what Christ did: be willing to take on the sins of the world, and thus transform them (and you).

The point is fairly simple: For the true Self, or the one Self, self and other can be easily exchanged; since both are equal, it makes no difference to the only Self. Conversely, if we cannot exchange self for other, then we are locked out of one-Self awareness, locked out of pure nondual awareness. Our unwillingness to take on the suffering of others locks us into our own suffering, with no escape, because it locks us into our self, period. As William Blake put it, "Lest the Last Judgment come and find me unannihilate, and I be seized and given unto the hands of my own selfhood."

A strange thing begins to happen when one practices *tonglen* for any length of time. First of all, nobody actually gets sick. I know of no bona fide cases of anyone getting ill because of *tonglen*, although a lot of us have used that fear as an excuse not to practice it. Rather, you find that you stop recoiling in the face of suffering, both yours and others'. You stop running from pain, and instead find that you can begin to transform it by simply being willing to take it into yourself and then release it. The real changes start to happen in you, by the simple willingness to get your ego-protecting tendencies out of the way. You begin to relax the self/other tension, realizing that there is only one Self feeling all pain or enjoying all success. Why get envious of others, when there is only one Self enjoying the success? This is why the "positive" side of *tonglen* is expressed in the saying: I rejoice in the merit of others. It's the same as mine, in nondual awareness. A great "equality consciousness" develops, which undercuts pride and arrogance on the one hand, and fear and envy on the other.

When the Mahayana path of compassion is established, when the exchangeability of self and other is realized, at least to some degree, then one is ready for the Vajrayana path. The Vajrayana is based on one uncompromising principle: There is only Spirit. As one continues to undercut the subject/object duality in all its forms, it increasingly becomes obvious that all things, high or low, sacred or profane, are fully and equally perfect manifestations or ornaments of Spirit, of Buddha-mind. The entire manifest universe is recognized as a play of one's own awareness, empty, luminous, clear, radiant, unobstructed, spontaneous. One learns not so much to seek awareness as to delight in it, play with it, since there is only awareness. Vajrayana is the path of playing with awareness, with energy, with luminosity, reflecting the perennial wisdom that the universe is a play of the Divine, and you (and all sentient beings as such) *are* the Divine.

The Vajrayana path therefore has three main divisions. In the first (the outer tantras), you visualize Deity in front of you or on top of your head, and you imagine healing energy and light raining down and into you, conferring blessings and wisdom. This is, of course, the psychic level, where one first establishes a communion with Deity.

In the second division (the lower inner tantras), you visualize yourself as the Deity and you repeat certain syllables or mantras that represent divine speech. This is the subtle level, the level of establishing union with Divinity. And then finally, in the third division (the higher inner tantras, Mahamudra and Maha-ati), one dissolves both self and Deity in pure unmanifest emptiness, the causal level of the supreme identity. At this point, the practice no longer involves visualization or mantra recitation or concentration, but rather the realization that your own awareness, just as it is, is always already enlightened. Since all things are *already* Spirit, there is no way to *reach* Spirit. There is only Spirit in all directions, and so one simply rests in the spontaneous nature of the mind itself, effortlessly embracing all that arises as ornaments of one's own primordial experience. The unmanifest and the manifest, or emptiness and form, unite in the pure nondual play of one's own awareness—generally regarded as the ultimate state that is no state in particular.

[GRACE AND GRIT: 246–50]

One Hand Clapping

You know the Zen koan, "What is the sound of one hand clapping?" Usually, of course, we need two hands to clap—and that is the structure of typical experience. We have a sense of ourselves as a subject in here, and the world as an object out there. We have these "two hands" of experience, the subject and the object. And typical experience is a smashing of these two hands together to make a commotion, a sound. The object out there smashes into me as a subject, and I have an experience—the two hands clap together, and experience emerges.

And so the typical structure of experience is like a punch in the face. The ordinary self is the battered self—it is utterly battered by the universe "out there." The ordinary self is a series of bruises, of scars, the results of these two hands of experience smashing together. This bruising is called *duhkha*, suffering. As Krishnamurti used to say, in that gap between the subject and the object lies the entire misery of humankind.

But with the nondual state, suddenly there are not two hands. Suddenly, the subject and the object are one hand. Suddenly, there is nothing outside of you to smash into you, bruise you, torment you.

Suddenly, you do not *have* an experience, you *are* every experience that arises, and so you are instantly released into all space: you and the entire Kosmos are one hand, one experience, one display, one gesture of great Perfection. There is nothing outside of you that you can want, or desire, or seek, or grasp—your soul expands to the corners of the universe and embraces all with infinite delight. You are utterly full, utterly saturated, so full and saturated that the boundaries to the Kosmos completely explode and leave you without date or duration, time or location, awash in an ocean of infinite care. You are released into the All, as the All—you are the self-seen radiant Kosmos, you are the universe of One Taste, and the taste is utterly infinite.

So what is the sound of that one hand clapping? What is the taste of that One Taste? When there is *nothing outside of you* that can hit you, hurt you, push you, pull you—what is the sound of that one hand clapping?

See the sunlight on the mountains? Feel the cool breeze? What is not utterly obvious? Who is not already enlightened? As a Zen master put it, "When I heard the sound of the bell ringing, there was no I and no bell, just the ringing." There is no twiceness, no twoness, in immediate experience! No inside and no outside, no subject and no object—just immediate awareness itself, the sound of one hand clapping.

So you are not in here, on this side of a transparent window, looking at the Kosmos out there. The transparent window has shattered, your bodymind drops, you are free of that confinement forever, you are no longer "behind your face" looking at the Kosmos—you simply are the Kosmos. You *are* all that. Which is precisely why you can swallow the Kosmos and span the centuries, and nothing moves at all. The sound of this one hand clapping is the sound the Big Bang made. It is the sound of supernovas exploding in space. It is the sound of the robin singing. It is the sound of a waterfall on a crystal-clear day. It is the sound of the entire manifest universe—and you are that sound.

Which is why your original face is not *in here*. It is the sheerest Emptiness or transparency of this shimmering display. If the Kosmos is arising, you are that. If nothing arises, you are that. In either case, you are that. In either case, you are not in here. The window has shattered. The gap between the subject and object is gone. There is no twiceness, no twoness, to be found anywhere—the world is *never* given to you *twice*, but always only once—and you are that. You are that One Taste.

This state is not something you can *bring about*. This nondual state, this state of One Taste, is the very nature of every experience *before* you slice it up. This One Taste is not some experience you bring about through effort; rather, it is the actual condition of all experience *before* you do anything to it. This uncontrived state is prior to effort, prior to grasping, prior to avoiding. It is the real world *before* you do anything to it, including the effort to "see it nondually."

So you don't have to do something special to awareness or to experience in order to make it nondual. It starts out nondual, its very nature is nondual—prior to any grasping, any effort, any contrivance. If effort arises, fine; if effort doesn't arise, fine; in either case, there is only the immediacy of One Taste, prior to effort and non-effort alike.

So this is definitely not a state that is hard to get into, but rather one that is impossible to avoid. It has always been so. There has never been a moment when you did not experience One Taste—it is the only constant in the entire Kosmos, it is the only reality in all of reality. In a million billion years, there has never been a single second that you weren't aware of this Taste; there has never been a single second where it wasn't directly in your Original Face like a blast of arctic air.

Of course, we have often lied to ourselves about this, we have often been untruthful about this, the universe of One Taste, the primordial sound of one hand clapping, our own Original Face. And the nondual traditions aim, not to bring about this state, because that is impossible, but simply to *point it out* to you so that you can no longer ignore it, no longer lie to yourself about who you really are.

[A BRIEF HISTORY OF EVERYTHING: 229–31]

You Are Already Aware

THE ESSENCE OF DZOGCHEN (or Maha-ati) is radically simple, and is in accord with the highest teachings of other of the world's great wisdom traditions, particularly Vedanta Hinduism and Ch'an (early Zen) Buddhism. In a nutshell: If Spirit has any meaning, it must be omnipresent, or all-pervading and all-encompassing. There can't be a place Spirit is not, or it wouldn't be infinite. Therefore, Spirit has to be completely present, right here, right now, in your own awareness. That is, your own present awareness, precisely as it is, without changing it or altering it in any way, is perfectly and completely permeated by Spirit.

Furthermore, it is not that Spirit is present but you need to be enlightened in order to see it. It is not that you are one with Spirit but just don't know it yet. Because that would also imply that there is some place Spirit is not. No, according to Dzogchen, you are always already one with Spirit, and that awareness is always already fully present, right now. You are looking directly at Spirit, with Spirit, in every act of awareness. There is nowhere Spirit is not.

Further, if Spirit has any meaning at all, then it must be eternal, or without beginning or end. If Spirit had a beginning in time, then it would be strictly temporal, it would not be timeless and eternal. And this means, as regards your own awareness, that you cannot become enlightened. You cannot attain enlightenment. If you could attain enlightenment, then that state would have a beginning in time, and so it would not be true enlightenment.

Rather, Spirit, and enlightenment, has to be something that you are fully aware of right now. *Something you are already looking at right now.* When I was receiving these teachings [from His Holiness Pema Norbu Rinpoche], I thought of the old puzzles in the Sunday supplement section of the newspaper, where there is a landscape and the caption says, "The faces of twenty famous people are hidden in this landscape. Can you spot them?" The faces were maybe Walter Cronkite, John Kennedy, that kind of thing. The point is that you are looking right at the faces. You don't need to see *anything* more in order to be looking at the faces. They are completely entering your visual field already, you just don't recognize them. If you still can't find them, then somebody comes along and simply points them out.

It's the same way with Spirit or enlightenment, I thought. We are all already looking directly at Spirit, we just don't recognize it. We have all the necessary cognition, but not the recognition. This is why the Dzogchen teachings don't particularly recommend meditation, useful as that may be for other purposes. Because meditation is an attempt to change cognition, to change awareness, and that is unnecessary and beside the point. Spirit is already completely and fully present in the state of awareness that you have now; nothing needs to be changed or altered. And, indeed, the attempt to change awareness is like trying to paint in the faces in the puzzle instead of simply recognizing them.

And thus, in Dzogchen, the central teaching is not meditation, because meditation aims at a change of state, and enlightenment is not a change of state but the recognition of the nature of any present state. Indeed, much of the teaching of Dzogchen centers on why meditation doesn't work, on why enlightenment can never be gained because it is always already present. Trying to get enlightenment would be like trying to attain your feet. The first rule in Dzogchen: There is nothing you can try to do, or try not to do, to get basic awareness, because it already and fully is.

Instead of meditation, then, Dzogchen uses what are called "the pointing-out instructions." Here the Master simply talks to you, and points out that aspect of your awareness that is *already* one with Spirit and has always been one with Spirit, that part of your awareness that is timeless and eternal, that is beginningless, that has been with you even before your parents were born (as Zen would put it). In other words, it's just like pointing out the faces in the puzzle. You don't have to change the puzzle or rearrange it, you only have to recognize that which you are already looking at. Meditation rearranges the puzzle; Dzogchen doesn't touch a thing. Thus the pointing-out instructions usually begin, "Without correcting or modifying your present awareness in any way, notice that . . ."

I cannot give the actual instructions, as those are the special province of the Dzogchen Master. But I can give you the Vedanta Hindu version, since they are already in print, particularly in the writings of the illustrious Sri Ramana Maharshi. As I would word it:

The one thing we are always already aware of is . . . awareness itself. We already have basic awareness, in the form of the capacity to Witness whatever arises. As an old Zen Master used to say, "You hear the birds? You see the sun? Who is not enlightened?" None of us can even imagine a state where basic awareness is not, because we would still be aware of the imagining. Even in dreams we are aware. Moreover, these traditions maintain, there are not two different types of awareness, enlightened versus ignorant. There is only awareness. And this awareness, exactly and precisely as it is, without correction or modification at all, is itself Spirit, since there is nowhere Spirit is not.

The instructions, then, are to recognize awareness, recognize the Witness, recognize the Self, and abide as that. Any attempt to get awareness is totally beside the point. "But I still don't see Spirit!" "You are aware of your not seeing Spirit, and that awareness is itself Spirit!"

You can practice mindfulness, because there is forgetfulness; but you cannot practice awareness, because there is only awareness. In mindfulness, you pay attention to the present moment. You try to "be here now." But pure awareness is the present state of awareness before you try to do *anything* about it. Trying to "be here now" requires a future moment in which you will then be mindful; but pure awareness is this moment before you try anything. You are already aware; you are already enlightened. You might not be always already mindful, but you are always already enlightened.

The pointing-out instructions go on like this, sometimes for a few minutes, sometimes for a few hours, sometimes for a few days, until you "get" it, until you recognize your own True Face, the "face you had before your parents were born" (that is, timeless and eternal, prior to birth and death). And it is a recognition, not a cognition. It's like peering into the window of a department store and seeing a vague figure staring back at you. You let the figure come into focus, and with a shock realize that it's your own reflection in the window. The entire world, according to these traditions, is nothing but the reflection of your own Self, reflected in the mirror of your own awareness. See? You are already looking right at it.

Thus, according to these traditions, basic awareness is not hard to reach, it's impossible to avoid, and the so-called "paths" to the Self are really obstacle courses. They prevent the recognition as long as they are engaged. There is only the Self, there is only God. As Ramana himself put it:

> There is neither creation nor destruction,
> Neither destiny nor free will;
> Neither path nor achievement;
> This is the final truth.

[GRACE AND GRIT: 370–72]

One Taste

PEOPLE MAKE TWO common mistakes on the way to One Taste. The first occurs in contacting the Witness, the second occurs in moving from the Witness to One Taste itself.

The first mistake: In trying to contact the Witness (or I-I), people imagine that they will *see something*. But you don't see anything, you simply rest as the Witness of all that arises—you are the pure and empty Seer, *not anything that can be seen*. Attempting to see the Seer as a special light, a great bliss, a sudden vision—those are all *objects*, they are not the Witness that you are. Eventually, of course, with One Taste, you will be *everything* that you see, but you cannot start trying to do that—trying to see the Truth—because that is what blocks it. You have to start with *neti, neti*: I am not this, I am not that.

So the first mistake is that people sabotage the Witness by trying to make it an object that can be grasped, whereas it is simply the Seer of all objects that arise, and it is "felt" only as a great background sense of Freedom and Release *from* all objects.

Resting in that Freedom and Emptiness—and impartially witnessing all that arises—you will notice that the *separate-self* (or ego) simply arises in consciousness *like everything else*. You can actually feel the self-contraction, just as you can feel your legs, or feel a table, or feel a rock, or feel your feet. The self-contraction is a feeling of interior tension, often localized behind the eyes, and anchored in a slight muscle tension throughout the bodymind. It is an effort and a sensation of contracting in the face of the world. It is a subtle whole-body tension. Simply notice this tension.

Once people have become comfortable resting as the empty Witness, and once they notice the tension that is the self-contraction, they imagine that to finally move from the Witness to One Taste, they have to get rid of the self-contraction (or get rid of the ego). Just that is the second mistake, because it actually locks the self-contraction firmly into place.

We assume that the self-contraction hides or obstructs Spirit, whereas in fact it is simply a radiant manifestation of Spirit itself, like absolutely every other Form in the universe. All Forms are not other than Emptiness, including the form of the ego. Moreover, the only thing that wants to get rid of the ego is the ego. Spirit loves everything that arises, just as it is. The Witness loves everything that arises, just as it is. The Witness loves the ego, because the Witness is the impartial mirror-mind that equally reflects and perfectly embraces *everything* that arises.

But the ego, convinced that it can become even more entrenched, decides to play the game of getting rid of itself—simply because, *as long as it is playing that game*, it obviously continues to exist (who else is playing the game?). As Chuang Tzu pointed out long ago, "Is not the desire to get rid of the ego itself a manifestation of ego?"

The ego is not a thing but a subtle *effort*, and you cannot use effort to get rid of effort—you end up with two efforts instead of one. The ego itself is a perfect manifestation of the Divine, and it is best handled by resting in Freedom, not by trying to get rid of it, which simply increases the effort of ego itself.

And so, the practice? When you rest in the Witness, or rest in I-I, or rest in Emptiness, simply notice the self-contraction. Rest in the Witness, and feel the self-contraction. When you feel the self-contraction, you are *already* free of it—you are already *looking at it*, instead of identifying with it. You are looking at it from the position of the Witness, which is always already free of all objects in any case.

So rest as the Witness, and feel the self-contraction—just as you can feel the chair under you, and feel the earth, and feel the clouds floating by in the sky. Thoughts float by in the mind, sensations float by in the body, the self-contraction hovers in awareness—and you effortlessly and spontaneously witness them all, equally and impartially.

In that simple, easy, effortless state, while you are *not* trying to get rid of the self-contraction but simply feeling it—and while you are therefore resting as the great Witness or Emptiness that you are—One Taste might more easily flash forth. There is nothing that you can do to bring about (or cause) One Taste—it is always already fully present, it is not the result of temporal actions, and you have never lost it anyway.

The most you can do, by way of temporal effort, is to avoid these two major mistakes (don't try to see the Witness as an object, just rest in the Witness as Seer; don't try to get rid of the ego, just feel it), and that will bring you to the edge, to the very precipice, of your own Original Face. At that point it is, in every way, out of your hands.

Rest as the Witness, feel the self-contraction: that is exactly the space in which One Taste can most easily flash forth. Don't do this as a strategic effort, but randomly and spontaneously throughout the day and into the night, standing thus always on the edge of your own shocking recognition.

So here are the steps:

Rest as the Witness, feel the self-contraction. As you do so, notice that the Witness is *not* the self-contraction—it is aware of it. The Witness is free of the self-contraction—and *you are the Witness.*

As the Witness, you are free of the self-contraction. *Rest in that* Freedom, Openness, Emptiness, Release. Feel the self-contraction, and let it be, just as you let all other sensations be. You don't try to get rid of the clouds, the trees, or the ego—just let them all be, and relax in the space of Freedom that you are.

From that space of Freedom—and at some unbidden point—you may notice that the feeling of Freedom has no inside and no outside, no center and no surround. Thoughts are floating in this Freedom, the sky is floating in this Freedom, the world is arising in this Freedom, and you are That. The sky is your head, the air is your breath, the earth is your skin—it is all that close, and closer. You are the world, as long as you rest in this Freedom, which is infinite Fullness.

This is the world of One Taste, with no inside and no outside, no subject and no object, no in here versus out there, without beginning and without end, without ways and without means, without path and without goal. And this, as Ramana said, is the final truth.

That is what might be called a "capping exercise." Do it, not instead of, *but in addition to,* whatever other practice you are doing—centering prayer, vipassana, prayer of the heart, zikr, zazen, yoga, etc. All of these other practices train you to enter a specific state of consciousness, *but One Taste is not a specific state*—it is compatible with any and all states, just as wetness is fully present in each and every wave of the ocean. One wave may be bigger than another wave, but it is not wetter. One Taste is the wetness of the water, not any particular wave, and therefore specific practices, such as prayer or vipassana or yoga, are *powerless* to introduce you to One Taste. All specific practices are designed to get you to a particular wave—usually a Really Big Wave—and that is fine. But One Taste is the wetness of even the smallest wave, so any wave of awareness you have right now is fine. Rest with that wave, feel the self-contraction, and stand Free.

But continue your other practices, first, because they will introduce you to specific and important waves of your own awareness (psychic, subtle, and causal), which are all important vehicles of your full manifestation as Spirit. Second, precisely because One Taste is too simple to believe and too easy to reach by effort, most people will never notice that the wave they are now on is wet. They will never notice the Suchness of their own present state. They will instead dedicate their lives to wave hopping, always looking for a Bigger and Better wave to ride—and frankly, that is fine. But keep the day job (your regular spiritual practice).

Those typical spiritual practices, precisely by introducing you to subtler and subtler *experiences,* will inadvertently help you *tire of experience altogether.* When you tire of wave jumping, you will stand open to the wetness or Suchness of whatever wave you are on. The pure Witness itself is *not an experience,* but the opening or clearing in which all experiences come and go, and as long as you are chasing experiences, including spiritual experiences, you will never rest as the Witness, let alone fall into the ever-present ocean of One Taste. But tiring of experiences, you will rest as the Witness, and it is as the Witness that you can notice Wetness (One Taste).

And then the wind will be your breath, the stars the neurons in your brain, the sun the taste of the morning, the earth the way your body feels. The Heart will open to the All, the Kosmos will rush into your soul, you will arise as countless galaxies and swirl for all eternity. There is only self-existing Fullness left in all the world, there is only self-seen Radiance here in Emptiness—etched on the wall of infinity, preserved for all eternity, the one and only truth: there is *just this,* snap your fingers, nothing more.

[ONE TASTE: October 31]

Translation versus Transformation

IN A SERIES of books (e.g., *A Sociable God, Up from Eden,* and *The Eye of Spirit*), I have tried to show that religion itself has always performed two very important, but very different, functions. One, it acts as a way of creating meaning for the separate self: it offers myths and stories and narratives and rituals and revivals that, taken together, help the separate self make sense of, and endure, the slings and arrows of outrageous fortune.

This function of religion does not usually or necessarily change the level of consciousness in a person; it does not deliver radical transformation. Nor does it deliver a shattering liberation from the separate self altogether. Rather, it consoles the self, fortifies the self, defends the self, promotes the self. As long as the separate self believes the myths, performs the rituals, mouths the prayers, or embraces the dogma, then the self, it is fervently believed, will be "saved"—either now in the glory of being God-saved or Goddess-favored, or in an afterlife that insures eternal wonderment.

But two, religion has also served—in a usually very, very small minority—the function of radical transformation and liberation. This function of religion does not fortify the separate self, but utterly shatters it—not consolation but devastation, not entrenchment but emptiness, not complacency but explosion, not comfort but revolution—in short, not a conventional bolstering of consciousness but a radical transmutation and transformation at the deepest seat of consciousness itself.

There are several different ways that we can state these two important functions of religion. The first function—that of creating meaning for the self—is a type of horizontal movement; the second function—that of transcending the self—is a type of vertical movement (higher or deeper, depending on your metaphor). The first I have named translation; the second, transformation.

With translation, the self is simply given a new way to think or feel about reality. The self is given a new belief—perhaps holistic instead of atomistic, perhaps forgiveness instead of blame, perhaps relational instead of analytic. The self then learns to translate its world and its being in the terms of this new belief or new language or new paradigm, and this new and enchanting translation acts, at least temporarily, to alleviate or diminish the terror inherent in the heart of the separate self.

But with transformation, the very process of translation itself is challenged, witnessed, undermined, and eventually dismantled. With typical translation, the self (or subject) is given a new way to think about the world (or objects); but with radical transformation, the self itself is inquired into, looked into, grabbed by its throat and literally throttled to death.

Put it one last way: with horizontal translation—which is by far the most prevalent, widespread, and widely shared function of religion—the self is, at least temporarily, made happy in its grasping, made content in its enslavement, made complacent in the face of the screaming terror that is in fact its innermost condition. With translation, the self goes sleepy into the world, stumbles numbed and near-sighted into the nightmare of samsara, is given a map laced with morphine with which to face the world. And this, indeed, is the common condition of a religious humanity, precisely the condition that the radical or transformative spiritual realizers have come to challenge and to finally undo.

For authentic transformation is not a matter of belief but of the death of the believer; not a matter of translating the world but of transforming the world; not a matter of finding solace but of finding infinity on the other side of death. The self is not made content; the self is made toast.

Now, although I have obviously been favoring transformation

and belittling translation, the fact is that, on the whole, both of these functions are incredibly important and altogether indispensable. Individuals are not, for the most part, born enlightened. They are born in a world of sin and suffering, hope and fear, desire and despair. They are born as a self ready and eager to contract; a self rife with hunger, thirst, tears, and terror. And they begin, quite early on, to learn various ways to translate their world, to make sense of it, to give meaning to it, and to defend themselves against the terror and the torture never lurking far beneath the happy surface of the separate self.

And as much as we, as you and I, might wish to transcend mere translation and find an authentic transformation, nonetheless translation itself is an absolutely necessary and crucial function for the greater part of our lives. Those who cannot translate adequately, with a fair amount of integrity and accuracy, fall quickly into severe neurosis or even psychosis: the world ceases to make sense—the boundaries between the self and the world are not transcended but instead begin to crumble. This is not breakthrough but breakdown; not transcendence but disaster.

But at some point in our maturation process, translation itself, no matter how adequate or confident, simply ceases to console. No new beliefs, no new paradigm, no new myths, no new ideas, will staunch the encroaching anguish. Not a new belief for the self, but the transcendence of the self altogether, is the only path that avails.

Still, the number of individuals who are ready for such a path is, always has been, and likely always will be, a very small minority. For most people, any sort of religious belief will fall instead into the category of consolation: it will be a new horizontal translation that fashions some sort of meaning in the midst of the monstrous world. And religion has always served, for the most part, this first function, and served it well.

I therefore also use the word *legitimacy* to describe this first function (the horizontal translation and creation of meaning for the separate self). And much of religion's important service is to provide legitimacy to the self—legitimacy to its beliefs, its paradigms, its worldviews, and its way in the world. This function of religion to provide a legitimacy for the self and its beliefs—no matter how temporary, relative, nontransformative, or illusory—has nonetheless been the single greatest and most important function of the world's religious traditions. The capacity of a religion to provide horizontal meaning, legitimacy, and sanction for the self and its beliefs—that function of religion has historically been the single greatest "social glue" that any culture has.

And one does not tamper easily, or lightly, with the basic glue that holds societies together. Because more often than not, when that glue dissolves—when that translation dissolves—the result, as we were saying, is not breakthrough but breakdown, not liberation but social chaos.

Where translative religion offers legitimacy, transformative religion offers authenticity. For those few individuals who are ready—that is, sick with the suffering of the separate self, and no longer able to embrace the legitimate worldview—then a transformative opening to true authenticity, true enlightenment, true liberation, calls more and more insistently. And, depending upon your capacity for suffering, you will sooner or later answer the call of authenticity, of transformation, of liberation on the lost horizon of infinity.

Transformative spirituality does not seek to bolster or legitimate any present worldview at all, but rather to provide true authenticity by shattering what the world takes as legitimate. Legitimate consciousness is sanctioned by the consensus, adopted by the herd mentality, embraced by the culture and the counterculture both, promoted by the separate self as the way to make sense of this world. But authentic consciousness quickly shakes all of that off of its back, and settles instead into a glance that sees only a radiant infinity in the heart of all souls, and breathes into its lungs only the atmosphere of an eternity too simple to believe.

Transformative spirituality, authentic spirituality, is therefore revolutionary. It does not legitimate the world, it breaks the world; it does not console the world, it shatters it. And it does not render the self content, it renders it undone.

[ONE TASTE: February 11]

Contemplating Art

WHEN I DIRECTLY VIEW, say, a great Van Gogh, I am reminded of what all superior art has in common: the capacity to simply take your breath away. To literally, actually, make you inwardly gasp, at least for that second or two when the art first hits you, or more accurately, first enters your being: you swoon a little bit, you are slightly stunned, you are open to perceptions that you had not seen before. Sometimes, of course, it is much quieter than that: the work seeps into your pores gently, and yet you are changed somehow, maybe just a little, maybe a lot; but you are changed.

No wonder that for the East and West alike, until just recent times, art was often associated with profound spiritual transformation. And I don't mean merely "religious" or "iconographic" art.

Some of the great modern philosophers, Schelling to Schiller to Schopenhauer, have all pinpointed a major reason for great art's power to transcend. When we look at any beautiful object (natural or artistic), we suspend all other activity, and we are simply aware, we only want to contemplate the object. While we are in this contemplative state, we do not want anything from the object; we just want to contemplate it; we want it to never end. We don't want to eat it, or own it, or run from it, or alter it: we only want to look, we want to contemplate, we never want it to end.

In that contemplative awareness, our own egoic grasping in time comes momentarily to rest. We relax into our basic awareness. We rest with the world as it is, not as we wish it to be. We are face to face with the calm, the eye in the center of the storm. We are not agitating to change things; we contemplate the object as it is. Great art has this power, this power to grab your attention and suspend it: we stare, sometimes awestruck, sometimes silent, but we cease the restless movement that otherwise characterizes our every waking moment.

It doesn't matter what the actual content of the art is; not for this. Great art grabs you, against your will, and then suspends your will. You are ushered into a quiet clearing, free of desire, free of grasping, free of ego, free of the self-contraction. And through that opening or clearing in your own awareness may come flashing higher truths, subtler revelations, profound connections. For a moment you might even touch eternity; who can say otherwise, when time itself is suspended in the clearing that great art creates in your awareness?

You just want to contemplate; you want it never to end; you forget past and future; you forget self and same. The noble Emerson: "These roses under my window make no reference to former roses or to better ones; they are for what they are; they exist with God today. There is no time for them. There is simply the rose; it is perfect in every moment of its existence. But man postpones or remembers; he does not live in the present, but with reverted eye laments the past, or heedless of the riches that surround him, stands on tiptoe to foresee the future. He cannot be happy and strong until he too lives with nature in the present, above time."

Great art suspends the reverted eye, the lamented past, the anticipated future: we enter with it into the timeless present; we are with God today, perfect in our manner and mode, open to the riches and the glories of a realm that time forgot, but that great art reminds us of: not by its content, but by what it does in us: suspends the desire to be elsewhere. And thus it undoes the agitated grasping in the heart of the suffering self, and releases us—maybe for a second, maybe for a minute, maybe for all eternity—releases us from the coil of ourselves.

That is exactly the state that great art pulls us into, no matter what the actual content of the art itself—bugs or Buddhas, landscapes or abstractions, it doesn't matter in the least. In this particular regard—from this particular context—great art is judged by its capacity to take your breath away, take your self away, take time away, all at once.

And whatever we mean by the word "spirit"—let us just say, with Tillich, that it involves for each of us our ultimate concern—it is in that simple awestruck moment, when great art enters you and changes you, that spirit shines in this world just a little more brightly than it did the moment before.

[THE EYE OF SPIRIT: 134–36]

Was Carl Jung a Mystic?

_____

J UNG FOUND THAT modern men and women can spontaneously
   produce virtually all of the main themes of the world's mythic
religions; they do so in dreams, in active imagination, in free association, and so on. From this he deduced that the basic mythic
forms, which he called archetypes, are common in all people, are
inherited by all people, and are carried in what he called the collective unconscious. He then made the claim that, and I quote, "mysticism is experience of the archetypes."

In my opinion there are several crucial errors in that view. One,
it is definitely true that the mind, even the modern mind, can spontaneously produce mythic forms that are essentially similar to the
forms found in mythic religions. The pre-formal stages of the
mind's development, particularly pre-operational and concrete operational thought, are myth-producing by their very nature. Since
all modern men and women pass through those stages of development in childhood, of course all men and women have spontaneous
access to that type of mythic thought-producing structure, especially in dreams, where primitive levels of the psyche can more
easily surface. But there's nothing mystical about that. Archetypes,
according to Jung, are basic mythic forms devoid of content; mysticism is _formless_ awareness. There's no point of contact.

Second, there is Jung's whole use of the word "archetype," a
notion he borrowed from the great mystics, such as Plato and Augustine. But the way Jung uses the term is _not_ the way those mystics
use the term, nor in fact the way mystics the world over use that

concept. For the mystics—Shankara, Plato, Augustine, Eckhart, Garab Dorje, and so on—archetypes are the first subtle forms that appear as the world manifests out of formless and unmanifest Spirit. They are the patterns upon which all other patterns of manifestation are based. From the Greek *arche typon*, original pattern. Subtle, transcendental forms that are the first forms of manifestation, whether that manifestation is physical, biological, mental, whatever. And in most forms of mysticism, these archetypes are nothing but radiant patterns or points of light, audible illuminations, brilliantly colored shapes and luminosities, rainbows of light and sound and vibration—out of which, in manifestation, the material world condenses, so to speak.

But Jung uses the term as certain basic mythic structures that are collective to human experience, like the trickster, the shadow, the Wise Old Man, the ego, the persona, the Great Mother, the anima, the animus, and so on. These are not so much transcendental as they are existential. They are simply facets of experience that are common to the *everyday* human condition. I agree that those mythic forms are collectively inherited in the psyche. And I agree entirely with Jung that it is very important to come to terms with those mythic "archetypes."

If, for example, I am having psychological trouble with my mother, if I have a so-called mother complex, it is important to realize that much of that emotional charge comes not just from my individual mother but from the Great Mother, a powerful image in my collective unconscious that is in essence the distillation of mothers everywhere. That is, the psyche comes with the image of the Great Mother embedded in it, just as the psyche comes already equipped with the rudimentary forms of language and of perception and of various instinctual patterns. If the Great Mother image is activated, I am not dealing with just my individual mother, but with thousands of years of the human experience with mothering in general, so the Great Mother image carries a charge and has an impact far beyond what anything my own mother could possibly do on her own. Coming to terms with the Great Mother, through a study of the world's myths, is a good way to deal with that mythic form, to make it conscious and thus differentiate from it. I agree entirely with Jung on that matter. But those mythic forms have nothing to do with mysticism, with genuine transcendental awareness.

Let me explain it more simply. Jung's major mistake, in my opinion, was to confuse collective with transpersonal (or mystical). Just because my mind inherits certain collective forms does not mean those forms are mystical or transpersonal. We all collectively inherit ten toes, for example, but if I experience my toes I am not having a mystical experience! Jung's "archetypes" have virtually nothing to do with genuinely spiritual, transcendental, mystical, transpersonal awareness; rather, they are collectively inherited forms that distill some of the very basic, everyday, existential encounters of the human condition—life, death, birth, mother, father, shadow, ego, and so on. Nothing mystical about it. Collective, yes; transpersonal, no.

There are collective prepersonal, collective personal, and collective transpersonal elements; and Jung does not differentiate these with anything near the clarity that they demand, and this skews his entire understanding of the spiritual process, in my opinion.

So I agree with Jung that it is very important to come to terms with the forms in both the personal and the collective mythic unconscious; but neither one of those has much to do with real mysticism, which is first, finding the light beyond form; then, finding the formless beyond light.

[GRACE AND GRIT: 180–82]

The Real Archetypes

FROM THE NEOPLATONIC traditions in the West, to the Vedanta and Mahayana and Trikaya traditions in the East, the real archetypes are subtle seed-forms upon which all of manifestation depends. In deep states of contemplative awareness, one begins to understand that the entire Kosmos emerges straight out of Emptiness, out of primordial Purity, out of *nirguna* Brahman, out of the Dharmakaya, and the first Forms that emerge out of this Emptiness are the basic Forms upon which all lesser forms depend for their being.

Those Forms are the actual archetypes, a term which means "original pattern" or "primary mold." There is a Light of which all lesser lights are pale shadows, there is a Bliss of which all lesser joys are anemic copies, there is a Consciousness of which all lesser cognitions are mere reflections, there is a primordial Sound of which all lesser sounds are thin echoes. Those are the real archetypes.

When we find those types of statements in Plotinus or Asanga or Garab Dorje or Abhinavigupta or Shankara, rest assured that those are not simply theoretical hunches or metaphysical postulates. Those are direct experiential disclosures issuing directly from the subtle dimension of reality, *interpreted* according to the *backgrounds* of those individuals, but *issuing* from this profound ontological reality, this subtle worldspace.

And if you want to know what these men and women are actually talking about, then you must take up the contemplative practice or injunction or paradigm, and perform the experiment yourself. These archetypes, the true archetypes, are a meditative experience, and you cannot understand these archetypes without performing the experiment. They are not images existing in the mythic worldspace, they are not philosophical concepts existing in the rational worldspace; they are meditative phenomena existing in the subtle worldspace.

So this experiment will disclose these archetypal data, and then you can help interpret what they mean. And by far the most commonly accepted interpretation is, you are looking at the basic forms and foundations of the entire manifest world. You are looking directly into the Face of the Divine. As Emerson said, bid the intruders take the shoes off their feet, for here is the God within.

[A BRIEF HISTORY OF EVERYTHING: 217–18]

Academic Religion

WHEN I WAS a youngster, and being the mad scientist type, I used to collect insects. Central to this endeavor was the killing jar. You take an empty mayonnaise jar, put lethal carbon tetrachloride on cotton balls, and place them in the bottom of the jar. You then drop the insect—moth, butterfly, whatnot—into the jar, and it quickly dies, but without being outwardly disfigured. You then mount it, study it, display it.

Academic religion is the killing jar of Spirit.

[ONE TASTE: November 24]

The Value of Polemics

ROBERT MCDERMOTT, in his essay "The Need for Dialogue in the Wake of Ken Wilber's *Sex, Ecology, Spirituality*," raises the issue of whether polemical discourse is ever appropriate for academic and especially spiritual dialogue. He ends up rather strongly condemning polemic, his major point being that it isn't "spiritual." But I believe that this reflects an impoverished and narrow view of spirit—what it is, and where it is located.

McDermott asks if we would ever hear polemic from the great spiritual philosophers, such as Aurobindo or James or Plotinus. The answer, of course, is yes. In fact, the vast majority of spiritual philosophers have engaged at one time or another in intense polemical discourse—Plato, Hegel, Kierkegaard, Nietzsche, Fichte, Schopenhauer, Schelling, Augustine, Origen, Plotinus, to name a very few. They do so, I believe, precisely because they understand the difference between what Chögyam Trungpa Rinpoche used to call "compassion" and "idiot compassion." This is perhaps the hardest lesson to learn in politically correct America, where idiot compassion—the abdication of discriminating wisdom and the loss of the moral fiber to voice it—is too often equated with "spirituality."

I think, on the contrary, that we admire these spiritual philosophers because idiot compassion was foreign to them, because they all had the moral courage to speak out in the most acerbic of terms when necessary, to make the hard calls and make them loud and clear. People too often imagine that "choiceless awareness" means making no judgments at all. But that itself is a judging activity.

Rather, "choiceless awareness" means that both judging and no judging are allowed to arise, appropriate to circumstances. I think this is exactly why so many great spiritual philosophers engaged in such incredibly *intense* polemic, Plotinus being a quite typical example. Plotinus so aggressively attacked the astrologers that Dante felt it necessary to consign the entire lot of them to the eighth ring of hell, and he unrelentingly tore into the Gnostics as having "no right to even speak of the Divine."

I used to think that if somebody engaged in that type of forceful polemic, they couldn't be very enlightened. I see now it is exactly the opposite. We tend to believe genuine spirituality should avoid all that, whereas in fact it quite often engages it passionately as a manifestation of its capacity to judge depth (i.e., its capacity for discriminating wisdom). Plotinus's acerbic and occasionally sarcastic attack on the astrologers and Gnostics is paradigmatic: they were a politically powerful and unpleasant lot, and it took courage to claim they had no right to even speak of the Divine. If McDermott is sincere about his pronouncements, then he would have been there to publicly condemn Plotinus, no doubt; but the point is that right or wrong, Plotinus stood up to be counted, and it is a service to us that he did so in no uncertain terms. Moreover, Plotinus is not saying one thing in public and another in private; you know exactly where he stands.

The question is thus not whether these great spiritual philosophers engaged in polemic, for they did; the question is why. When such sages engage in intense polemic, I suppose we sometimes get nothing but their lingering neurosis; but we often get the full force of the overall judgment of their entire being, a shout from the heart in a sharp scream. It takes no effort at all to act out the former; it takes enormous courage to stand up and voice the latter, and this is what I have come to admire in all the sages and philosophers I mentioned who have left us the full force of their summary judgments.

Contrary to McDermott's sincere but misplaced pronouncements, such polemic comes not from this, but from the other, side of equanimity. One Taste is the ground of intense judgments, not their abdication. These are not lunatics blathering prejudices; more like what the Tibetans would call the wrathful aspect of enlightened awareness.

McDermott tells us that he used to publicly and passionately voice his own judgments of qualitative distinctions and discriminating wisdom, but that he quit doing so in order to become a better administrator. I accept his choice. But I think it would be catastrophic for everybody in the transpersonal field to adopt that same stance and abdicate the public voicing of their discriminating wisdom.

There are many who see all too clearly the sad shape our field is in. They talk about it often in private. They tell me about it all the time. They are truly alarmed by the reactionary, antiprogressive, and regressive fog thickly creeping over the entire field. Yet most of them are not willing to stand up and be counted, precisely because the countercultural police await, poised and ready to sanctimoniously damn them. A little less administrative juggling, and a little more discriminating wisdom backed with occasional polemic, is exactly what the entire field could use, in my opinion. I, at any rate, can no longer sit by and smile numbly as depth takes a vacation. And in a more honest process, where our public pronouncements actually match our private statements, we just might find that spiritual awareness includes, not excludes, the fiercest of judgments.

[THE EYE OF SPIRIT: 276–79]

Sleep, Dreams, and Dreamless Sleep

THE SLEEP CYCLE is fascinating. The body goes to sleep, and that leaves only the subtle (mind and soul) and the causal (formless Witness). So as the body goes to sleep, the subtle mind and soul appear vividly in dreams, visions, images, and occasionally archetypal illuminations. At some point the subtle goes to sleep—the mind goes to sleep, the soul goes to sleep—and that leaves only formlessness, or deep dreamless sleep, which is actually the Witness or primordial Self in its own naked nature, with no objects of any sort. (This procession from gross to subtle to causal is the evolutionary or ascending arc.)

At some point during the deep dreamless state, the soul stirs, awakens, and emerges from its sleep in formlessness, and dreaming once again begins. Since the limitations and restrictions of the gross body are not present in the dream state, the subtle mind and soul can express their deepest wishes (to merely think or wish a thing is to see it materialize instantly in the dream)—which is why prophets, saints, sages, and depth psychologists have always given so much attention to dreams: a deeper self is speaking here, so for goodness' sake, pay attention. Shankara, Freud, and Jimminy Cricket all agree: "A dream is a wish your heart makes, when you're fast asleep."

As the dream state comes to a close (there are often several cycles between subtle-dreaming and causal-dreamless), then the gross body begins to stir, and the subtle mind is slowly submerged as the gross egoic orientation and the gross body awaken from their slumber. The body wakes up, the ego wakes up (the gross ego and gross body are interlinked)—in short, the frontal personality wakes up—and the person remembers very little, if anything, of the extraordinary tour that just occurred. (That movement from causal to subtle to gross is the involutionary or descending arc.)

Each "waking up" in that descending arc—when the subtle awakens and begins to dream, then the gross awakens and begins to perceive—is accompanied, in the usual individual, with a forgetting, an anamnesis. In the deep dreamless state, individuals revert to their pure formless Self, but when the subtle arises, they forget the Self and identify with the soul, with luminosities and images and ecstatic visions—they are lost in the dream state, already mistaking it for reality. Then, as the gross ego-body awakens from its slumber in the dream, it generally forgets most of that subtle state itself, unless it struggles to remember a particular dream, which is only a fragment of the wonders of the subtle. Instead, the gross ego-body looks out upon the sensorimotor world—the smallest world of all—and takes that for ultimate reality. It has forgotten both its causal Self and its subtle soul, and it sees merely the gross and the sensorimotor. It has lost its Spirit and lost its soul and damn near lost its mind, and what is left it proudly calls reality.

(Incidentally, that sequence: gross dissolving into subtle dissolving into causal, upon which, if there are karmas present, causal giving rise to subtle giving rise to gross, whereupon one "awakens" to find oneself trapped in a gross body in a gross world: just that is the same sequence described in the *Tibetan Book of the Dead*, for that sequence is said to be identical in the process of death [gross dissolves into subtle dissolves into causal] and rebirth [causal gives rise to subtle gives rise to gross, with a "forgetting" at each step]. To consciously master the waking-dreaming-sleeping cycle is therefore said to be the same as being able to *consciously* choose one's rebirth: to master one is to master the other, for they are identical cycles through the Great Nest of Being, gross to subtle to causal and back again. Even so, that cycle, however exalted, is nothing but the cycle of *samsara,* of the endless rounds of torturous birth and death. Mastering that cycle is, at best, an aid to the ultimate goal: the recognition of One Taste. For only in One Taste does one step off that brutal cycle altogether, there to rest as the All. Neither gross nor subtle nor causal are the ultimate estate, which is the simple Feeling of Being, the simple Feeling of One Taste.)

Most individuals, then, have forgotten their own higher states—forgotten their soul, forgotten their Self, forgotten the One and Only Taste. But as consciousness becomes a little stronger—through growth, through meditation, through evolution—then the transitions between the three great states are not met with blacking out or forgetting or anamnesis. At first, consciousness will be able to maintain access to a stable witnessing awareness, or mirror-mind, for large portions of the gross waking state. When you then fall asleep at night, a fairly stable witnessing will tend to persist into the dream state, and you will lucid-dream. (Actually, I distinguish between lucid dreaming and pellucid dreaming. In lucid dreaming, there is usually a tendency to play out egoic impulses in the dream: you imagine orgies, fame, food, flying, whatever turns your ego on. In pellucid dreaming, you simply remain as the witness, as the mirror-mind, which, by definition, does not alter anything that arises, but simply witnesses it. The dream will still arise, and it will be driven by your own desires and karmas, but you will merely and pellucidly witness it.)

At this point, as you pass from the subtle dream into the causal formless, you will probably "black out" or cease to remain conscious, even though you are reverting to your own highest Self. You will probably regain consciousness when the subtle emerges and dreaming resumes; you will pellucid-dream. As awareness becomes yet stronger, there is a point where a tiny interior tension is dissolved—it's hard to describe—and a very, very subtle awareness will persist into deep dreamless sleep. This is the beginning of the capacity for constant consciousness, or unbroken access to the mirror-mind through all changes of state. Resting as this causal, formless awareness (or pure Emptiness), "you" will "perceive" (there is no you nor ordinary perception) the dream state emerge out of your own formless awareness; you will witness the dream state as long as it persists, and then, as the body begins to awaken, you will perceive the gross realm arise out of your own subtle awareness. Thus you will directly perceive the causal produce the subtle produce the gross, and so it will become obvious why the entire universe is a manifestation of the One True and Formless Self, or pure Emptiness, which is identical in all sentient beings without exception.

This constant access to the pure Witness (which is called "the fourth state," after the other three of waking, dreaming, and sleeping) nonetheless still retains a subtle dualism: the formless Witness, on the one hand, witnesses objects, on the other. The Absolute Subject serenely and with unshakable equanimity witnesses the entire world of objects. That subtle split between subject and object, inside and outside, formless and form, is undone when the Witness shatters and One Taste is recognized as always-already present (this is called *turiyatita,* or the fifth and final state that transcends and includes the other four). At first this recognition is a peak experience; then a plateau experience, eventually recognized through all three states; then a permanent adaptation or realization, the realization that there has never been anything but One Taste, the purest Emptiness that is one with the entire world of Form. Arhats have the Formless, the ordinary have Form, Buddhas have both in One Taste.

In the most general sense, "constant consciousness" refers to both constant Witnessing through all three states and constant One Taste through all three states, although the latter, of course, is the culminating nondual realization. The "experiential" difference between constant Witnessing and constant One Taste is roughly this: you are no longer witnessing all that arises, you simply *are* all that arises. And it "feels" that way. In Witnessing, there is a capacity to deploy *attention*: a tiny root tension underlies attention, for it is a subtle contraction in the field of nondual awareness (and it feels that way: to concentrate is to focus, narrow, restrain). But there is no attention in One Taste, for one is not focused on this to the exclusion of that. There is simply everything that is arising, and you are that, through all changes of state. (Of course, if attention and concentration are required, you can certainly do that within the space of One Taste; it's just that, *in* itself, One Taste is without contraction, attention, or concentration, for it floats freely as all that is.)

Thus, with One Taste, the tiny interior tension that is Witnessing uncoils in the vast expanse of All Space. The entire universe exists in the simple feeling of Being, which is your own estate, with no inside and no outside, for those have meaning only to the bounded, separate self. You are not looking at anything; you simply are everything that arises, so that you disperse to the ends of infinity. With constant One Taste, you "feel" your "oneness" with everything in the gross, in the subtle, and in the causal, as they arise and pass. You do not arise and pass; you are eternally unmovable, as the simple feeling of Being, as always-already One Taste, which is the pure Emptiness and radical Freedom that is one with all Form forever.

With constant Witnessing, you gain your first real Release from the world, because you are no longer its victim but its Witness. With One Taste you recognize a deeper Release, which is that you are free of the entire world because you *are* the entire world. This, again, is the great truth in Shankara's (and Ramana's) statement:

> The world is illusory;
> Brahman alone is real;
> Brahman is the world.

"The world is illusory; Brahman alone is real" is constant Witnessing. "Brahman is the world" is constant One Taste. But you must go through them in that order, because otherwise you will take any peak experience in the gross realm and think you've gotten the ultimate Nondual, so you will end up championing the most superficial forms of oneness, and condemning those that are in fact much deeper.

But even the smallest glimmer of One Taste and your world will never be the same. You will inhale galaxies with every breath and sleep as the stars all night. Suns and moons and glorious novas will rush and rumble through your veins, your heart will pulse and beat in time with the entire loving universe. And you will never move at all in this radiant display of your very own Self, for you will long ago have disappeared into the darkness of your noble night.

[ONE TASTE: November 30]

The Meaning of Illness

I N ANY DISEASE, a person is confronted with two very different entities. One, the person is faced with the actual disease process itself—a broken bone, a case of influenza, a heart attack, a malignant tumor. Call this aspect of disease "illness." Cancer, for example, is an illness, a specific disease with medical and scientific dimensions. Illness is more or less value-free; it's not true or false, good or bad, it just is—just like a mountain isn't good or bad, it just is.

But two, the person is also faced with how his or her society or culture deals with that illness—with all the judgments, fears, hopes, myths, stories, values, and meanings that a particular society hangs on each illness. Call this aspect of disease "sickness." Cancer is not only an illness, a scientific and medical phenomenon; it is also a sickness, a phenomenon loaded with cultural and social meanings. Science tells you when and how you are ill; your particular culture or subculture tells you when and how you are sick.

This is not necessarily or even especially a bad thing. If a culture treats a particular illness with compassion and enlightened understanding, then sickness can be seen as a challenge, as a healing crisis and opportunity. Being "sick" is then not a condemnation or a moral judgment, but a movement in a larger process of healing and restoration. When sickness is viewed positively and in supportive terms, then illness has a much better chance to heal, with the concomitant result that the entire person may grow and be enriched in the process.

Men and women are condemned to meaning, condemned to creating values and judgments. It is not enough to know *that* I have a disease; *that I* have a disease is my illness. But I also need to know *why* I have that disease. Why me? What does it mean? What did I do wrong? How did this happen? I need, in other words, to attach some sort of *meaning* to this illness. And for this meaning I am dependent first and foremost on my society, on all the stories and values and meanings in which my culture dresses a particular disease. My sickness, as opposed to my illness, is defined largely by the society—the culture or subculture—in which I find myself.

Consider, for example, gonorrhea. As an illness it is fairly straightforward: an infection chiefly of the mucosal lining of the genitourinary tract, spread by sexual contact among infected partners, and highly sensitive to treatment by antibiotics, especially penicillin. That's gonorrhea as an illness, as a medical entity. But our society attaches a great number of meanings and judgments to gonorrhea as a sickness—society has much to say about the disease and those who contract it, some of which is true, much of which is false and cruel. Those who contract gonorrhea are unclean, or perverts, or morally degenerate; gonorrhea is a moral disease, which is its own painful punishment; those who get gonorrhea deserve it, since they are morally unfit—and so on.

Long after penicillin has destroyed the illness, the sickness may still remain, its judgments and condemnations eating away at the person's soul the way the simpler bacteria once ate at the body. "I'm a rotten person, I'm no good, how horrible of me. . . ."

Thus, it is through science that I seek to explain my illness (in this *case,* a genitourinary infection caused by *Neisseria gonorrheae*), but it is through my society that I seek to *understand* my sickness—what does it mean? (In this case, it means you are morally defective.) Whatever culture or subcultures I belong to will offer up an entire battery of meanings and judgments for my sickness, and to the extent that I am in a particular culture, then that culture's meanings and judgments are in me, internalized as part of the very fabric of how I will understand myself and my sickness. And the point is that the meaning of that sickness—negative or positive, redemptive or punitive, supportive or condemnatory—can have an enormous impact on me and on the course of my disease: the sickness is often more destructive than the illness.

Most disturbing is the fact that when society judges a sickness to be "bad," when it judges a sickness negatively, it almost always does so exclusively out of fear and ignorance. Before it was understood that gout is a hereditary disease, it was ascribed to moral weakness. A blameless illness became a *guilt-ridden sickness,* simply through *lack of accurate scientific* information. Likewise, before it was understood that tuberculosis is caused by the tubercle bacillus, it was thought to be a process of "consumption," whereby a person with weak character was slowly "consumed." A bacterial illness became a sickness indicative of a weak character. And even earlier, plagues and famines were thought to be a direct intervention of a vengeful God, punitive retribution for the collective sins of a particular people.

Condemned to meaning: we would much prefer to be saddled with a harmful and negative meaning than to have no meaning at all. And so whenever illness strikes, society is on hand with a huge supply of readymade meanings and judgments through which the individual seeks to understand his or her sickness. And when that society is in fact ignorant of the true cause of an illness, this ignorance usually breeds fear, which in turn breeds negative judgments about the character of the person unlucky enough to come down with the illness. The person is not only ill but sick, and this sickness, defined by society's judgments, all too often becomes a self-fulfilling and self-reinforcing prophecy: Why me? Why am I sick? Because you've been bad. But how do you know I've been bad? Because you're sick.

In short, the less the actual medical causes of an illness are understood, then the more it tends to become a sickness surrounded by desultory myths and metaphors; the more it tends to be treated as a sickness due to character weakness or moral flaws of the afflicted individual; the more it is misunderstood as a sickness of the soul, a personality defect, a moral infirmity.

Now of course there are cases when moral weakness or weakness of will (say, a refusal to stop smoking) or personality factors (say, depression) can contribute directly to illness. Mental and emotional factors can most definitely play a significant role in some illnesses. But this is entirely different from an illness with major medical causes being wholly misinterpreted, through ignorance and lack of information, as caused by moral defect or weakness. This is a simple case of society's trying to understand a disease by condemning a soul.

Now cancer is a disease, an illness, about which very little is actually known (and there is virtually nothing known about how to cure it). And therefore, cancer is a disease around which an enormous number of myths and stories have grown up. As an illness, cancer is poorly understood. As a sickness, it has assumed awesome proportions. And as difficult as the illness of cancer is, the sickness of cancer is absolutely overwhelming.

So the first thing you have to understand when you get cancer is that almost all the information you will receive is shot through with myths. And because medical science has so far largely failed to explain the cause and cure of cancer, it—the medical establishment—is itself infected with an enormous number of myths and falsehoods.

To give only one example: The National Cancer Association claims in its national advertising that "half of all cancers are now curable." Fact: In the last forty years there has been no significant increase whatsoever in the average survival rates of cancer patients—despite the much vaunted "war on cancer" and the introduction of more sophisticated radiation techniques, chemotherapies, and surgeries. All of that has had no significant impact on cancer survival rates at all. (The one happy exception is the blood cancers—Hodgkin's and leukemia—which respond well to chemotherapy. The pathetic 2 percent or so increase in survival rates for the remaining cancers are due almost entirely to early detection; the rest of the cancer rates have not budged an inch, literally.) And as for breast cancer, the survival rates have actually gone down!*

Now, doctors know this. They know the statistics. And on rare

*New York Times, April 24, 1988: "Statistics released recently suggest that,

occasions you can get a doctor to admit it. . . . So what's a typical doctor to do? He knows that his medical interventions—surgery, chemotherapy, radiation—are ultimately not very effective, and yet he has got to do something. And so this is what he does: Since he can't really control the illness, he attempts to control the sickness. That is, he attempts to define the meaning of the disease by prescribing a certain way that the patient should think about the cancer—namely, that the disease is an entity that the doctor understands and that the doctor can medically treat, and that other approaches are useless or even harmful.

In practice, this means that the doctor will, for example, sometimes prescribe chemotherapy *even when he knows it won't work.* In a highly respected and authoritative text on cancer—*The Wayward Cell* by Dr. Victor Richards—the author presents a long discussion of why, under many circumstances, chemotherapy doesn't work, and then he goes on to state that nonetheless under the same circumstances chemotherapy should still be prescribed. Why? Because, he says, it "keeps the patient oriented toward the proper medical authorities." Put bluntly, it stops the patient from looking elsewhere for treatment—it keeps the patient oriented toward orthodox medicine, whether or not that medicine actually works in this case.

Now that is not treating the illness; that is treating the sickness—it is attempting to control how the patient understands the disease and therefore the types of treatment the patient will seek. The point is that the treatments might not significantly affect the illness, but they do affect the sickness, or how one *orients oneself* toward the illness: the types of authorities one will listen to and the types of medicines one will accept.

A good friend who had advanced cancer was given the very strong recommendation, by her doctors, that she undertake yet another course of very intensive chemotherapy. If she did so,

---

far from winning the war on breast cancer, we may actually be losing ground. . . . Women over 50 survive the disease no longer today than they did a decade ago, and women under 50 had a 5 percent greater mortality rate in 1985 than in 1975."

the doctors told her, she could expect to live an average of twelve months. It finally dawned on her to ask: How long can I be expected to live without the chemotherapy? The answer came back: Fourteen months. The doctors' recommendation: Do the chemotherapy. (People who haven't actually gone through something like this have a very hard time understanding that these kinds of things happen all the time—which is testament to just how thoroughly we have accepted the orthodox medical interpretation and "treatment" of the sickness.)

I really don't blame doctors for this; they are largely helpless in the face of desperate patient expectations. Nor have I ever met a single doctor that I thought was maliciously trying to manipulate patients. By and large these physicians are incredibly decent men and women doing the very best they can in impossible circumstances. They're as helpless as we are. It's simply that, whereas illness is a fairly clearcut scientific entity, sickness is a religion. Since cancer the illness is largely unresponsive, doctors are forced to try to treat cancer the sickness, at which point they must act more like priests than like scientists, a role they are ill-equipped and ill-trained to play. But in a democracy of the sick, the high priest is the doctor, by popular demand.

And so this is the point that I began with: a lot of information that decent doctors will give you about cancer is shot through with myths, simply because they are forced to act not just as doctors but also as priests, as manipulators of the *meaning* that your illness has. They are dispensing not just science but religion. Follow their treatments and you will be saved; go elsewhere for treatment and you will be damned.

In seeking treatments for the cancer that Ken's wife, Treya, had been diagnosed with, the couple pored through mountains of literature, which conveyed not only "facts" about cancer but all the meanings and judgments that society assigns to it:

And it wasn't just the general society at large that supplied various stories. Treya and I were exposed to several different cultures and subcultures, each of which had something very definite to say. Here are just a few:

1. *Christian:* The fundamentalist message: Illness is basically a punishment from God for some sort of sin. The worse the illness, the more unspeakable the sin.

2. *New Age:* Illness is a lesson. You are giving yourself this disease because there is something important you have to learn from it in order to continue your spiritual growth and evolution. Mind alone causes illness and mind alone can cure it. A yuppified postmodern version of Christian Science.

3. *Medical:* Illness is fundamentally a biophysical disorder, caused by biophysical factors (from viruses to trauma to genetic predisposition to environmental triggering agents). You needn't worry about psychological or spiritual treatments for most illnesses, because such alternative treatments are usually ineffectual and may actually prevent you from getting the proper medical attention.

4. *Karma:* Illness is the result of negative karma; that is, some nonvirtuous past actions are now coming to fruition in the form of a disease. The disease is "bad" in the sense that it represents past nonvirtue; but it is "good" in the sense that the disease process itself represents the burning up and the purifying of the past misdeed; it's a purgation, a cleansing.

5. *Psychological:* As Woody Allen put it, "I don't get angry; I grow tumors instead." The idea is that, at least in pop psychology, repressed emotions cause illness. The extreme form: Illness as death wish.

6. *Gnostic:* Illness is an illusion. The entire manifest universe is a dream, a shadow, and one is free of illness only when one is free from illusory manifestation altogether, only when one awakens from the dream and discovers instead the One reality beyond the manifest universe. Spirit is the only reality, and in Spirit there is no illness. An extreme and somewhat off-centered version of mysticism.

7. *Existential:* Illness itself is without meaning. Accordingly it can

take any meaning I *choose* to give it, and I am solely responsible for these choices. Men and women are finite and mortal, and the authentic response is to accept illness as part of one's finitude even while imbuing it with personal meaning.

8. *Holistic:* Illness is a product of physical, emotional, mental, and spiritual factors, none of which can be isolated from the others, none of which can be ignored. Treatment must involve all of these dimensions (although in practice this often translates into an eschewal of orthodox treatments, even when they might help).

9. *Magical:* Illness is retribution. "I deserve this because I wished So-and-so would die." Or, "I better not excel too much, something bad will happen to me." Or, "If too many good things happen to me, something bad has to happen." And so on.

10. *Buddhist:* Illness is an inescapable part of the manifest world; asking why there is illness is like asking why there is air. Birth, old age, sickness, and death—these are the marks of this world, all of whose phenomena are characterized by impermanence, suffering, and selflessness. Only in enlightenment, in the pure awareness of nirvana, is illness finally transcended, because then the entire phenomenal world is transcended as well.

11. *Scientific:* Whatever the illness is, it has a specific cause or cluster of causes. Some of these causes are determined, others are simply random or due to pure chance. Either way, there is no "meaning" to illness, there is only chance or necessity.

Men and women necessarily and intrinsically swim in the ocean of meaning. Treya and I were about to drown in it.

[GRACE AND GRIT: 40–45, 46–47]

The Moment of Death

ALL OF THE GREAT wisdom traditions maintain that the actual moment of death is an extremely important and precious opportunity, and for this reason: At the moment of death, the person has dropped the gross physical body, and therefore the higher dimensions—the subtle and the causal—immediately flash in the deceased's awareness. If the person can recognize these higher and spiritual dimensions, then the person can acknowledge immediate enlightenment, and do so much more easily than when in the dense and obstructing physical body. . . . This explanation is based on the Tibetan system, which seems to be the most complete, but it is in essential agreement with the mystical traditions the world over.

The human being has three major levels or dimensions: gross (the body), subtle (the mind), and causal (spirit). During the dying process, the lower levels of the Great Chain dissolve first, starting with the body, starting with sensation and perception. When the body dissolves (ceases functioning), the subtler dimensions of mind and soul come to the fore, and then, at the actual moment of death, when all levels dissolve, pure causal Spirit flashes forth in the person's awareness. If the person can recognize this Spirit as his or her own true nature, then enlightenment is realized on the spot, and the person returns permanently to Godhead, as Godhead.

If recognition does not take place, then the person (the soul) enters the intermediate state, the *bardo*, which is said to last up to a few months. The subtle level emerges, and then eventually the gross level emerges, and the person is then reborn in a physical body to begin a new life, taking with them, in their soul, whatever wisdom and virtue (but not specific memories) they may have accumulated in the previous life.

Whatever we might think about the notion of reincarnation or the *bardo* or afterlife states, this much seems certain: If you at all believe that some part of you partakes of the divine, if you at all believe that you have access to some sort of Spirit that transcends your mortal body in any sense, then the moment of death is crucial, because at that point the mortal body is *gone,* and if there is *anything* that remains, this is the time to find out, yes?

[GRACE AND GRIT: 392–93]

The Ultimate Spiritual Test

D EATH: THE MYSTICS are unanimous that death contains the
secret to life—to eternal life, in fact. As Eckhart put it, echo-
ing the mystics everywhere: "No one gets as much of God as those
who are thoroughly dead." Or Ramana Maharshi: "You will know
in due course that your glory lies where you cease to exist. Or the
Zenrin: "While alive, live as a dead person, thoroughly dead."

They don't mean physically dead; they mean dead to the separate-self sense. And you can "test" your own spiritual awareness
in relation to death by trying to imagine the following items:

1. A famous Zen koan says, "Show me your Original Face, the
Face you had before your parents were born." This is not a trick
question or a symbolic question; it is very straightforward, with a
clear and simple answer. Your Original Face is simply the pure
formless Witness, prior to the manifest world. The pure Witness,
itself being timeless or prior to time, is equally present at all points
of time. So of course this is the Self you had before your parents
were born; it is the Self you had before the Big Bang, too. And it is
the Self you will have after your body—and the entire universe—
dissolves.

This Self existed prior to your parents, and prior to the Big Bang,
because it exists prior to time, period. And you can *directly* contact
the Self you had before your parents were born by simply resting
in the pure Witness *right now.* They are one and the same formless
Self, right now, and right now, and right now.

By "imagining" what you are like before your parents were

born, you are forced to drop all identity with your present body and ego. You are forced to find that in you which actually goes beyond you—namely, the pure, empty, formless, timeless Witness or primordial Self. To the extent you can actually rest as the timeless Witness ("I am not this, not that"), then you have died to the separate self—and discovered your Original Face, the face you had before your parents were born, before the Big Bang was born, before time was born. You have, in fact, found the great Unborn.

2. Similarly, imagine what the world will be like a hundred years after you die. You don't have to imagine specific details, just realize that the world will be going on a century after you are gone. Imagine that world without you. So many things will have changed—different people, different technologies, different cars and planes. . . . But *one thing will not have changed;* one thing will be the same: Emptiness, One Taste, Spirit. Well, you can taste that *right now.* One and the same formless Witness will look out from all eyes, hear with all ears, touch with all hands . . . the same formless Witness that is your own primordial Self right now, the same One Taste that is yours, right now, the same radiant Spirit that is yours, right now, the same radical Release that is yours, right now.

Were you somebody different a thousand years ago? Will you be somebody different a thousand years from now? What is this One Self that is forever your own deepest being? Must you believe the lies of time? Must you swallow the insanity that One Spirit does not exist? Can you right now show me your Original Face, of which there is One and Only One in all the entire World?

Please, I beg you, listen to Erwin Schroedinger, the Nobel-prize-winning cofounder of quantum mechanics, and how can I convince you that he means this literally?

"It is not possible that this unity of knowledge, feeling, and choice which you call *your own* should have sprung into being from nothingness at a given moment not so long ago; rather, this knowledge, feeling, and choice are essentially eternal and unchangeable and numerically one in all people, nay in all sensitive beings. The conditions for your existence are almost as old as the rocks. For thousands of years men have striven and suffered and begotten and women have brought forth in pain. A hundred years ago [there's the test], another man sat on this spot; like you he gazed with awe and yearning in his heart at the dying light on the glaciers. Like you he was begotten of man and born of woman. He felt pain and brief joy as you do. *Was* he someone else? Was it not you yourself?"

WAS IT NOT YOU, YOUR PRIMORDIAL SELF? Are you not humanity itself? Do you not touch all things human, because you are its only Witness? Do you not therefore love the world, and love all people, and love the Kosmos, because you are its only Self? Do you not weep when one person is hurt, do you not cry when one child goes hungry, do you not scream when one soul is tortured? You *know* you suffer when others suffer. You know this! "*Was* it someone else? Was it not you yourself?"

3. By thinking of what you were like a thousand years ago or a thousand years hence, you drop your identity with the present body and ego, and find that in you which goes beyond you— namely, the pure, formless, timeless Self or Witness of the entire World. And once every twenty-four hours you completely drop your egoic identity, not as a mere imaginative exercise but as a fact. Every night, in deep dreamless sleep, you are plunged back into the formless realm, into the realm of pure consciousness without an object, into the realm of the formless, timeless Self.

This is why Ramana Maharshi said, "That which is not present in deep dreamless sleep is not real." The Real must be present in all three states, including deep dreamless sleep, and the *only* thing that is present in all three states is the formless Self or pure consciousness. And each night you die to the separate-self sense, die to the ego, and are plunged back into the ocean of infinity that is your Original Face.

All three of those cases—the Self you had before your parents were born, the Self you will have a hundred years from now, and the Self you have in deep dreamless sleep—point to one and the same thing: the timeless Witness in you which goes beyond you, the pure Emptiness that is one with all Form, the primordial Self that embraces the All in radical One Taste. And That, which is *just this*, has not changed, will not change, will never change, because it never enters the corrupting stream of time with all its tears and terror.

The ultimate "spiritual test," then, is simply your relation to death (for all three of those cases are examples of death). If you want to know the "ultimate truth" of what you are doing right now, simply submit it to any of those tests. Practicing astrology? If it is not present in deep dreamless sleep, it is not real. Running with wolves? If it is not present a hundred years from now, it is not real. Care of the Soul? If it is not present in deep dreamless sleep, it is not real. Healing your inner child? If it was not present prior to your parents' birth, it is not real. You remember your reincarnated past lives? If it is not present in deep dreamless sleep, it is not real. Using diet for spiritual cleansing? If it is not present a hundred years from now, it is not real. Worshipping Gaia? If it is not present in deep dreamless sleep, it is not real.

All of those relative practices and translative beliefs are fine, but never forget they are secondary to the great Unborn, your Original Face, the Face of Spirit in all its radiant forms, the forms of your very own being and becoming, now and again, now and forever, always and already.

"*Was* it someone else? Was it not you yourself?"

[ONE TASTE: December 29]

Spiritual Unfolding

THERE ARE FOUR major stages of spiritual unfolding: belief, faith, direct experience, and permanent adaptation: you can believe in Spirit, you can have faith in Spirit, you can directly experience Spirit, you can become Spirit.

Those are the typical *stages* that people pass through as they grow and evolve into the higher levels or structures of consciousness. And the difference between basic *structures* and passing *stages*? The former are permanent acquisitions; the latter, temporary phases. Matter, body, mind, subtle-soul, and causal-spirit are all basic *structures of consciousness*: once they emerge, they tend to remain in existence as permanent capacities (even enlightened beings have physical bodies with which they eat and minds with which they can think; and they continue to enter the subtle-dream state, but they do so consciously—they still have subtle-level phenomena, but now seen from a higher level, the causal Witness and nondual One Taste).

But, during development, individuals go through various phases as the overall basic structures emerge, and these phases or stages tend to be temporary, passing, and transitional. We speak of the "toddler stage," for example, where the infant learns to walk using the body. Once the basic capacity of walking is acquired, the ability to walk permanently remains, but the toddler stage itself passes (adults who are still toddling are in trouble, drunk, or both). Basic structures and capacities remain, phases or stages pass.

We've already seen some of the basic structures of consciousness: matter, body, mind, soul (psychic and subtle), and spirit (causal and nondual)—which are simply the major levels in the Great Nest of Being. But as people grow and evolve into the higher levels of the Great Nest, they tend to go through four *phases* in their own spiritual understanding: belief, faith, experience, and adaptation.

1. Belief is the earliest (and therefore, the most common) stage of spiritual orientation. Belief originates at the mental level, generally, since it requires images, symbols, and concepts. But the mind itself goes through several transitional phases in its own development—magic, mythic, rational, and vision-logic—and *each of those is the basis of a type (and stage) of spiritual or religious belief.*

Magic belief is egocentric, with subject and object often fused, thus marked by the notion that the individual self can dramatically affect the physical world and other people through mental wishes, voodoo and sympathetic magic being the most well-known examples. *Mythic belief* (which is always sociocentric/ethnocentric, since different people have different myths that are mutually exclusive: if Jesus is the one and only savior of humankind, Krishna is kaput) invests its spiritual intuitions in one or more physically disembodied gods or goddesses, who have ultimate power over all human actions. *Rational belief*—to the extent that reason chooses to believe at all—attempts to *demythologize* religion and portray God or the Goddess, not as an anthropomorphic deity, but as an ultimate Ground of Being. This rationalization reaches it zenith with *vision-logic belief,* where sciences such as systems theory are often used to explain this Ground of Being as a Great Holistic System, Gaia, Goddess, Eco-Spirit, the Web of Life, and so forth.

All of those are mental beliefs, usually with strong emotional sentiments; but they are not necessarily direct experiences of supramental spiritual realities. As such, they are merely forms of translative belief: they can be embraced without changing one's present level of consciousness in the least. But as those merely translative gestures begin to mature, and as direct emergence of the higher domains increasingly presses against the self, mere beliefs give way to faith.

2. Faith begins when belief loses its power to compel. Sooner or later, *any* mental belief—precisely because it is mental and not supramental or spiritual—will begin to lose its forcefulness. For example, the mental belief in spirit as the Web of Life will begin to pale in its power to persuade: no matter how much you keep believing in the Web of Life, you still feel like a separate, isolated ego, beset with hope and fear. You try to believe harder, it still doesn't work. You spend five years believing really hard, yet you still feel like you, separate and alone. Mere belief might have provided you with a type of translative meaning, but not with an actual *transformation,* and this slowly, painfully, becomes obvious. It's even worse if you are involved in magic or mythic beliefs, because not only do these not transform you, they act as a regressive force in your awareness, moving you not toward, but away from, the transrational.

Still, there is occasionally a genuine, spiritual, transmental intuition behind the mental belief in Gaia or the Web of Life, namely, an intuition of the Oneness of Life. But this intuition cannot be fully realized as long as belief grips consciousness. For all *beliefs* are ultimately divisive and dualistic-holistic beliefs are ultimately just as dualistic as analytic beliefs, because both make sense only in terms of their opposites. You are not supposed to *think* the All, you are supposed to *be* the All, and as long as you are clinging to beliefs about the All, it will never happen. Mere beliefs are cardboard nutrition for the soul, spiritual empty calories, and sooner or later they cease to fascinate and console.

But usually between letting go of belief, on the one hand, and finding direct experience, on the other, the person is carried only by faith. If the belief in Oneness can no longer offer much consolation, still the person has faith that Oneness is there, somehow, calling out to him or her. And they are right. Faith soldiers on when belief becomes unbelievable, for faith hears the faint but direct calling of a higher reality—of Spirit, of God, of Goddess, of Oneness—a higher reality that, being beyond the mind, is *beyond belief.* Faith stands on the threshold of direct supramental, transrational experience. Lacking dogmatic beliefs, it has no sense of security; not yet having direct experience, it has no sense of certainty. Faith is thus a no-man's land—a thousand questions, no answers—it possesses only a dogged determination to find its spiritual abode, and, pulled on by its own hidden intuition, it will eventually find direct experience.

3. *Direct experience* decisively answers the nagging questions inherent in faith. There are usually two phases of direct experience: peak experiences and plateau experiences.

Peak experiences are relatively brief, usually intense, often unbidden, and frequently life-changing. They are actually "peek experiences" into the transpersonal, supramental levels of one's own higher potentials. Psychic peak experiences are a glimpse into nature mysticism (gross-level oneness); subtle peak experiences are a glimpse into deity mysticism (subtle-level oneness); causal peak experiences are a glimpse into emptiness (causal-level oneness); and nondual peak experiences are a glimpse into One Taste. As Roger Walsh has pointed out, the higher the level of the peak experience, the rarer it is. (This is why most experiences of "cosmic consciousness" are actually just a glimpse of nature mysticism or gross-level oneness, the shallowest of the mystical realms. Many people mistake this for One Taste, unfortunately. This confusion is epidemic in eco-theorists.)

Most people remain, understandably, at the stage of belief or faith (and usually magical or mythical at that). Occasionally, however, individuals will have a strong peak experience of a genuinely transpersonal realm, and it completely shatters them, often for the better, sometimes for the worse. But you can tell they aren't merely repeating a belief they read in a book, or giving merely translative chitchat: they have truly seen a higher realm, and they are never quite the same.

(This is not always a good thing. Someone at the concrete-literal mythic level, for example, can have a peak experience of, say, the subtle level, and the result is a reborn fundamentalist: their particular mythic god-figure is the *only* figure that can save the entire world, and they will burn your body to save your soul. Someone at the vision-logic level can have a psychic-level peak experience, and then their "new eco-paradigm" is the *only* thing that can save the planet, and they will gladly march lock-step in eco-fascism to save you from yourself. Religious fanaticism of such ilk is almost impossible to dismantle, because it is an intense mixture of higher truth with lower delusion. The higher truth is often a very genuine spiritual experience, a true "peek" experience of a higher domain; but precisely because it is a brief, temporary experience—and not an enduring, steady, clear awareness—it gets immediately snapped up and translated downward into the lower level, where it confers an almost unshakable legitimacy on even the loopiest of beliefs.)

Whereas peak experiences are usually of brief durations—a few minutes to a few hours—*plateau experiences* are more constant and enduring, verging on becoming a permanent adaptation. Whereas peak experiences can, and usually do, come spontaneously, in order to sustain them and turn them from a peak into a plateau—from a brief altered state into a more *enduring trait*—prolonged practice is required. Whereas almost anybody, at any time, at any age, can have a brief peak experience, I know of few bona fide cases of plateau experiences that did not involve years of sustained spiritual practice. Thus, whereas belief and faith are by far the most common types of spiritual orientation, and while peak experiences are rare but authentic spiritual experiences, from this point on in spiritual unfolding, we find only those who are involved in sustained, intense, prolonged, profound spiritual practice.

Plateau experiences, like peak experiences, can be of the psychic, subtle, causal, or nondual domains. I will give one example, taken from Zen, that covers all four. Typically, individuals practicing Zen meditation will start by counting the breaths, one to ten, repeatedly. When they can do that for half an hour without losing count, they might be assigned a koan (such as the syllable *mu*, which was my first koan). For the next three or four years, they will practice several hours each day, concentrating on the sound *mu* and attempting not to drop it (there is, simultaneously, an intense inquiry into "What is the meaning of *mu*?" or "Who is it that is concentrating on *mu*?"). Several times each year, they will attend seven-day *sesshins*, or intense practice sessions, where they will be encouraged to practice throughout the day and into the night.

The first important plateau experience occurs when students can uninterruptedly hold on to *mu* for most of their waking hours. *Mu* has become such a part of consciousness, such a part of you—in fact, you become *mu* uninterruptedly—that you can hold it in awareness, in an unbroken fashion, all day, literally. In other words, a type of witnessing awareness is now a *constant* capacity throughout the gross-waking state. Students are then told that if they truly want to penetrate *mu*, they must continue working on it even during their sleep. (When I first heard this, I thought it was a joke, a type of macho initiation humor, of the sort, "If you want to be part of the fighting First Infantry, Mister, you have to eat three live snakes." I thought they were just trying to scare me; they were actually trying to help.) Another two or three years, and dedicated students do indeed continue a subtle concentration on *mu* right into the dream state. There is now a *constant* witnessing awareness even in the subtle-dream realm. At this point, as students approach the causal unmanifest (or pure cessation), they are on the verge of the explosion known as satori, which is a breakthrough from the "frozen ice" of pure causal absorption to the Great Liberation of One Taste. At first, this One Taste is itself a peak experience, but it, too, will become, with further practice, a plateau experience, then a permanent adaptation.

4. *Adaptation* simply means a *constant, permanent access to a given level of consciousness.* Most of us have already adapted (or evolved) to matter, body, and mind. And some of us have had peak experiences into the transpersonal levels (psychic, subtle, causal, or nondual). But with actual practice, we can evolve into plateau experiences of these higher realms, and these plateau experiences, with further practice, can become permanent adaptations: constant access to psychic, subtle, causal, and nondual occasions—constant access to nature mysticism, deity mysticism, formless mysticism, and integral mysticism—all as easily available to consciousness as matter, body, and mind now are. And this is likewise evidenced in a constant consciousness (*sahaja*) through all three states—waking,

dreaming (or *savikalpa samadhi*), and sleeping (or *nirvikalpa samadhi*). It then becomes obvious why "That which is not present in deep dreamless sleep is not real." The Real must be *present in all* three states, including deep dreamless sleep, and pure Consciousness is the only thing that is present in all three. This fact becomes perfectly obvious when you rest as pure, empty, formless Consciousness and "watch" all three states arise, abide, and pass, while you remained Unmoved, Unchanged, Unborn, released into the pure Emptiness that is all Form, the One Taste that is the radiant All, eternally and forever.

"*Was* it somebody else? Was it not you yourself?"

Those are some of the major phases we tend to go through as we adapt to the higher levels of our own spiritual nature: *belief* (magic, mythic, rational, holistic); *faith* (which is an intuition, but not yet a direct experience, of the higher realms); *peak experience* (of the psychic, subtle, causal, or nondual—in no particular order, because peak experiences are usually one-time hits); *plateau experience* (of the psychic, subtle, causal, and nondual—almost always in that order, because competence at one stage is required for the next); and *permanent adaptation* (to the psychic, subtle, causal, and nondual, also in that order, for the same reason).

Several important points:

• You can be at a relatively high level of spiritual development and still be at a relatively low level in other lines (e.g., the deeper psychic can be progressing while the frontal is quite retarded). We all know people who are spiritually developed but still rather immature in sexual relations, emotional intimacy, physical health, and so on. Even if you have constant access to One Taste, that will not make your muscles grow stronger, will not necessarily get you that new job, won't get you the girl, and won't cure all your neurosis. You can still have deep pockets of shadow material that are not necessarily dug up as you advance into higher stages of spiritual practice or meditation (precisely because meditation is *not*, contra the popular view, an uncovering technique; if it were, most of our meditation teachers wouldn't need psychotherapy, whereas most all of them do, like everybody else. Meditation is not primarily *uncovering* the repressed unconscious, but allowing the *emergence* of higher domains—which usually leaves the lower, repressed domains still lower, and still repressed).

So even as you advance in your own spiritual unfolding, consider combining it with a good psychotherapeutic practice, because spiritual practice, as a rule, will not adequately expose the psychodynamic unconscious. Nor will it appropriately exercise the physical body—so try weightlifting. Nor will it exercise the pranic body—try adding t'ai chi ch'uan. Nor will it work with group or community dynamic, so add . . . Well, the point, of course, is to take up *integral practice* as the only sound and balanced way to proceed with one's own higher development.

• Even though many of those stages unfold in a specified sequence, nonetheless one's *overall* development (or self-development) follows no set pattern, no fixed stages, no rigid sequence. Overall development is an amalgam of dozens of different developmental lines, all of which develop relatively independently, so no overall pattern can be fixed: each individual will follow his or her own unique unfolding.

• Even though I have described higher stages whose access usually takes at least five or six years of arduous practice (and whose highest stages often take thirty years or more), don't let that put you off if you are a beginner. *Simply begin practice*—of course, five or six years will go by in a blink, but you will be reaping the abundant rewards. On the other hand, if you listen to those teachers who are selling nothing but beliefs (magic, mythic, rational, or holistic), you will be nothing but five or six years sadder. (Holistic beliefs are fine—and quite accurate—for the *mental* realm. But spirituality is about the *transmental* realm, the supramental realm, the superconscious realm, and no amount of mind translations will help you transcend the mind. And no amount of Person-Centered Civil Religion will deliver you from yourself.) Rather, you must take up a contemplative, transpersonal, supramental practice. So no matter how daunting practice seems, simply begin. As the old joke has it: How do you eat an elephant? One bite at a time.

• And the fact is, a few bites into the elephant and you will already start gaining considerable benefits. You might begin, say, twenty minutes a day of centering prayer, as taught by Father Thomas Keating. Many people report almost immediate effects— calming, opening, caring, listening: the heart melts a little bit, and so do you. *Zikr* for a half hour; *vipassana* for forty minutes; yoga exercises twice a day, worked into your schedule; tantric visualization; prayer of the heart; counting your breaths for fifteen minutes each morning before you get out of bed. Any of those are fine; whatever works for you, just take the first few bites. . . .

• We need to be gentle with ourselves, it is true; but we also need to be firm. Treat yourself with real compassion, not idiot compassion, and therefore begin to challenge yourself, engage yourself, push yourself: begin to practice.

• As any of these practices start to take hold, you might find it appropriate to attend an intensive retreat for a few days each year. This will give you a chance to extend the little "peeks" of practice into the beginning plateaus of practice. The years will go by, yes, but you will be ripening along with them, slowly but surely transcending the lesser aspects of yourself, and opening to the greater. There will come a day when you will look back on all that time as if it were just a dream, because in fact it is a dream, from which you will soon awaken.

• The point is simple: If you are interested in genuine transformative spirituality, find an authentic spiritual teacher and *begin practice*. Without practice, you will never move beyond the phases of belief, faith, and random peak experiences. You will never evolve into plateau experiences, nor from there into permanent adaptation. You will remain, at best, a brief visitor in the territory of your own higher estate, a tourist in your own true Self.

[ONE TASTE: December 30]

An Ounce of Laughter

<hr>

TRANSCENDENCE RESTORES HUMOR. Spirit restores humor. Suddenly, smiling returns. Too many representatives of too many movements—even many very good movements, such as feminism, environmentalism, meditation, spiritual studies—seem to lack humor altogether. In other words, they lack lightness, they lack a distance from themselves, a distance from the ego and its grim game of forcing others to conform to its contours. There is self-transcending humor, or there is the game of egoic power. No wonder Mencken wrote that "Every third American devotes himself to improving and lifting up his fellow citizens, usually by force; this messianic delusion is our national disease." We have chosen egoic power and politically correct thought police; grim Victorian reformers pretending to be defending civil rights; messianic new paradigm thinkers who are going to save the planet and heal the world. They should all trade two pounds of ego for one ounce of laughter.

[ONE TASTE: December 7]

Just This

I N THE HEART of Emptiness there is a mysterious impulse, mysterious because there is actually nothing in the heart of Emptiness (for there is nothing in Emptiness, period). Yet there it is, this mysterious impulse, the impulse to . . . create. To sing, to shine, to radiate; to send forth, reach out, and celebrate; to sing and shout and walk about; to effervesce and bubble over, this mysterious exuberance in the heart of Emptiness.

Emptiness empties itself of emptiness, and thus becomes Full, pregnant with all worlds, a fruition of the infinite impulse to play, hidden in the heart of your own deepest Self. If you rest in the Witness, settle back as I-I, and look very carefully for the Looker—if you turn within right now and try to see the Seer—you won't see anything at all, for you cannot see the Seer. All you will find is a vast Freedom and Emptiness, in which the entire Kosmos is now arising. Out of the pure Emptiness that is your deepest suchness, all worlds arise. Your own impulse of looking has brought forth the universe, and here it resides, in the vastness of all space, which is to say, in the purity of your own primordial awareness. This has been obvious all along; this you have known, all along. Just this, and nothing more, *just this*.

[ONE TASTE: July 31]

Books by Ken Wilber

An Annotated List

For each title the original date of publication appears in parentheses, followed by the facts of publication for the current or most recent edition.

The Spectrum of Consciousness (1977). Wheaton, Ill.: Quest, 1996 (2nd ed.).

> One of the founding texts of transpersonal psychology, this book introduced the full-spectrum model, the first to show, in a systematic way, how the great psychological systems of the West can be integrated with the great contemplative traditions of the East.

No Boundary: Eastern and Western Approaches to Personal Growth (1979). Boston: Shambhala Publications, 1985.

> A simple yet comprehensive guide to psychologies and therapies available from both Western and Eastern sources—from psychoanalysis to Zen, Gestalt to TM, existentialism to tantra. Wilber presents a map of human consciousness against which the various therapies are introduced and explained. Specific exercises are given in each chapter, designed to help the reader understand the nature and practice of each therapy.

The Spectrum of Consciousness and *No Boundary* have been designated by Wilber (in *The Eye of Spirit*) as "Wilber-1," the early "Romantic" phase of his work.

The Atman Project: A Transpersonal View of Human Development (1980). Wheaton, Ill.: Quest Books, 1996.

The first psychological system to suggest a way of uniting Eastern and Western, conventional and contemplative, orthodox and mystical approaches into a single, coherent framework, integrating views from Freud to Buddha, Gestalt to Shankara, Piaget to Yogachara, Kohlberg to Krishnamurti. Wilber outlines seventeen stages of development, including the *bardo* stages of preconception, prenatal, and postlife states.

Up from Eden: A Transpersonal View of Human Evolution (1981). Wheaton, Ill.: Quest Books, 1996.

Evolution as a magnificent journey of Spirit-in-action. In telling the story of humankind's growth, Wilber contends with a painful question: Men and women are said to be evolving toward God-consciousness—yet how can we speak of spiritual evolution in the face of modern atrocities such as Auschwitz, Hiroshima, and Chernobyl? Drawing on theorists from Jean Gebser to Jürgen Habermas, Wilber outlines the major waves of Spirit's historical unfolding.

The Atman Project and *Up from Eden* constitute "Wilber-2," the "evolutionary/developmental" phase of his work.

The Holographic Paradigm and Other Paradoxes: Exploring the Leading Edge of Science (1982) Boston: Shambhala Publications, 1985.

An anthology of contributions by prominent scientists and thinkers (such as Karl Pribram, Stanley Krippner, Renée Weber, William Irwin Thompson, David Bohm, Marilyn Ferguson, and others) on the dialogue between science and religion. Wilber's contributions include "Physics, Mysticism, and the New Holographic Paradigm: A Critical Appraisal" and "Reflections on the New-Age Paradigm: A Conversation with Ken Wilber" (both of which also appear in *Eye to Eye*).

A Sociable God: Toward a New Understanding of Religion (1983) Boston: Shambhala Publications, 1984.

This scholarly introduction to a psychology and sociology of religion presents a system of reliable methods by which to make testable judgments of the authenticity of any religious movement.

Eye to Eye: The Quest for the New Paradigm (1983) Boston: Shambhala Publications, 1996 (3rd ed.).

Wilber examines three realms of knowledge: the empirical realm of the senses, the rational realm of the mind, and the contemplative realm of the spirit. Includes important papers such as "The Pre/Trans Fallacy" and "A Mandalic Map of Consciousness."

Quantum Questions: Mystical Writings of the World's Great Physicists (1984). Boston: Shambhala Publications, 1985.

An anthology of nontechnical excerpts selected by Wilber from the mystical writings of great physicists: Heisenberg, Schroedinger, Einstein, de Broglie, Jeans, Planck, Pauli, and Eddington.

Transformations of Consciousness: Conventional and Contemplative Perspectives on Development, by Ken Wilber, Jack Engler, and Daniel P. Brown (1986). Boston: Shambhala Publications, 1986.

Nine essays from the *Journal of Transpersonal Psychology* by six writers (the three authors plus Mark Epstein, John Chirban, and Jonathan Lieff) exploring the full-spectrum model of human growth and development. Wilber's three chapters—"The Spectrum of Development," "The Spectrum of Psychopathology," and "Treatment Modalities"—represent the "Wilber-3" phase of his work (which first emerged in papers written in 1981), characterized by the distinction of the different developmental lines that unfold through the levels of the spectrum model.

Spiritual Choices: The Problems of Recognizing Authentic Paths to Inner Transformation, edited by Dick Anthony, Bruce Ecker, and Ken Wilber (1987). New York: Paragon House, 1987.

Transpersonal psychologists and spiritual teachers—including Frances Vaughan, John Welwood, Claudio Naranjo, Jacob Needleman, Werner Erhard, and Ram Dass—contribute to this study of religious movements, aimed at answering the seeker's dilemma of how to distinguish spiritual tyranny from legitimate spiritual authority. Wilber's contribution is "The Spectrum Model," an adaptation of "Legitimacy, Authenticity, and Authority in the New Religions" from *Eye to Eye*.

Grace and Grit: Spirituality and Healing in the Life and Death of Treya Killam Wilber (1991). Boston: Shambhala Publications, 1993.

The moving story of Ken's marriage to Treya and the five-year journey that took them through her illness (breast cancer), treatment, and eventual death. Ken's wide-ranging commentary is combined with Treya's personal journals. This book covers a period during which Wilber put his own work on hold as he became Treya's full-time support person.

Sex, Ecology, Spirituality: The Spirit of Evolution (1995). Boston: Shambhala Publications, 1995.

In over eight hundred pages, this tour de force of scholarship and vision traces the course of evolution from matter to life to mind, and describes the common patterns that evolution takes in all three domains. Wilber particularly focuses on the rise of modernity and postmodernity: what they mean, how they relate to gender issues, to psychotherapy, to ecological concerns, and to various liberation movements—and how the modern and postmodern world can even conceive of Spirit. Wilber-4 (the four-quadrants model).

This is the first volume of the projected *Kosmos Trilogy*. Volume 2 is tentatively titled *Sex, God, and Gender*. Volume 3 is tentatively subtitled *The Spirit of Post/Modernity*.

A Brief History of Everything (1996) Boston: Shambhala Publications, 1996.

A short, highly readable version of *Sex, Ecology, Spirituality*, written in an accessible, conversational style, without all the technical arguments and end notes.

The Eye of Spirit: An Integral Vision for a World Gone Slightly Mad (1997). Boston: Shambhala Publications, 1998.

Wilber uses his spectrum model to create an integral approach to such important fields as psychology, spirituality, anthropology, cultural studies, art and literary theory, ecology, feminism, and planetary transformation. Includes a historical summary of his own work and responses to his critics.

The Marriage of Sense and Soul: Integrating Science and Religion (1998) New York: Random House, 1998.

An original approach to the centuries-old problem of the relationship between science and religion. After surveying the world's great wisdom traditions and extracting features they all share, Wilber offers compelling arguments that are not only compatible with scientific truth, but share a similar scientific method. The result is an integration of science and religion that unites the best of ancient wisdom and modern knowledge.

One Taste: The Journals of Ken Wilber (1999) Boston: Shambhala Publications, forthcoming in January 1999.

A variety of writings are presented in journal format, including daily reflections, meditation experiences, and insights into current trends in spirituality and psychology.

Index

advaita (nonduality), 8
advaya (nonduality), 8
alaya (ultimate reality), 72
alayavijñana (causal realm), 42, 67, 72
All, transfinite nature of the, 64
Allen, Woody, 168
anandamayakosha (causal realm), 42, 67, 72
annamayakosha (physical realm), 41, 65, 70
archaic stage of development, 65, 70
archetypes
  Jung's definition of, 147–49
  original meaning of, 148
  as seed-forms, 150–51
art, contemplating, 144–46
ascending arc, 156
Atman project, 99–100
atomism, 61
Aurobindo, Sri, 105, 122
authenticity, transformative religion and, 143
awareness
  constancy of, 132–34
  choiceless, 153–54
  experiment, 75–77
  no-boundary, 22, 26
  Spirit as ever-present, 44–46

bardo (intermediate state), 170–71
Beauty, 104
belief, stage of spiritual unfolding, 177–78, 182
Benoit, Hubert, 121

bija-mantra, 67
biological level of consciousness, 41–43
Blake, William, 14, 126
bliss, following, 90–91
blocks
  dissolving, 80–84
  to feeling-attention in body, 77–78
  meaning of, 78–80
bodhisattva vow, vision-logic and, 93–94
body. *See also* structures of consciousness
  awareness experiment, 75–77
  blocks in, 77–84
  integral approach to, 102–4
  level of Great Chain of Being, 49
  limiting experience to the, 85–86
bodymind
  centaur as symbol of, 73–74
  healing the split, 75–84
Bohr, Niels, mysticism and, 16
breath, as vital force, 76–77
breathing exercise, for body awareness, 75–77
Broglie, Louis de, mysticism and, 16, 18
Broughton, James, 73
Buddha, 101
Buddhism
  Hinayana, 123–24
  Mahayana, 124–26
  Vajrayana, 126–27
Buddhist conception of cause of illness, 169

cancer, 165–69
Capra, Fritjof, 18–19
Catherine, Saint, 1

causal, the
    dreamless sleep and, 156–60
    level of consciousness, 41–43
    peak experiences, 179, 182
    stage of development, 67, 72, 110
    at time of death, 170–71
    structure of consciousness, 72
causation, downward and upward, 58
celestial orders, 55
centaur, symbol of bodymind integration,
    73–74
centering prayer, 184
chakras, stages of development and, 65–67
Chandogya Upanishad, 3
chemotherapy, efficacy of, 166–67
Chesterton, G. K., 123
choiceless awareness, 153–54
Christian conception of cause of illness,
    168
Chuang Tzu, 40, 136
concepts, contrasted with images and
    symbols, 70
consciousness. *See also* constant conscious-
    ness, Great Chain of Being
    levels of, 41–43
    nine basic structures of, 67–72
    seven stages and three realms, 65–67
    three states of, 21
    waves and streams in, 115–22
constant consciousness, 44–48
    during dreamless sleep, 158–59
    effect of awakening, 46–48
    as effect of permanent adaptation,
    181–182
contemplation, of art, 144–46
Coomaraswamy, Ananda, 4, 51
countercultural spirituality, 111, 112

death
    importance of moment of, 170–71
    spiritual awareness of, 172–75
deep ecology, 63, 111
deeper psychic personality system, 118–20
descending arc, 157
development. *See also* consciousness; Great
    Chain of Being; spectrum of
    consciousness; spiritual unfolding
    Buddhism and the stages of, 123–27
    cognitive and moral, 58, 59
    human, 96–98
    nine basic structures, pathologies, and
    treatments, 67–72

seven stages of, 65–67
    concurrent, of ego, soul, and Spirit, 121
    three realms of, 67
Dharma, 101
Dionysius the Areopagite, Saint, 55
direct experience, of the transpersonal,
    179–81, 182
disease. *See* illness
disidentification, from individual self,
    38–40
divine play, 1–2
divine schizophrenic, 46–47
downward causation, 58
dreamless sleep
    the causal and, 156–60
    the Witness and, 156–60, 174
dreams
    lucid and pellucid, 158
    the subtle and, 156–59
duality, 128–29
    the Witness and, 159
duhkha (suffering), 128
Dzogchen, 131–34
    meditation and, 132–33
    pointing-out instruction and, 132–34

Eckhart, Meister, 29, 30, 172
ecofeminism, 63, 111
ecophilosophy, 63
ecoprimitivism, 111
ecopsychology, 111
Eddington, Sir Arthur, mysticism and, 16,
    18, 19, 20
Edwards, Paul, 62
ego. *See also* self
    egolessness and, 31–35
    frontal personality system, 118–20
    "getting rid" of, 135–37
    indwelling spirit and, 3–4
    personality system development and,
    121–22
egolessness, ego and, 31–35
Einstein, Albert, mysticism and, 16, 17, 18,
    19–20
elephant, how to eat (joke), 183
elevationist movements, 90–91
Emerson, Ralph Waldo, 145, 151
    on the nature of self and soul, 9–11
emotion
    projection and suppression of, 78–80
    releasing blocks to, 80–84

emotional-sexual stage of development,
109
Emptiness, fullness of, 186
enlightenment, "unattainability" of,
131–32
evolution
cultural, 113
Great Chain of Being and, 113–14
spiritual, 98–99
evolutionary arc, 156
exercise. *See* breathing exercise; Witness
Exercise
existential conception of cause of illness,
168–69
existential structure of consciousness, 71
experience
body, mind, and spirit, 85–87
direct, of the transpersonal, 179–81, 182
duality and, 128
experiential, intellectual, and spiritual,
85–87
Eye of Spirit (Wilber), 105, 115

faith, stage of spiritual unfolding, 178–79,
182
fear, hostility and, 78–79
formal-reflexive structure of consciousness,
71
Freedom, 137–38
Freud, Sigmund, reducing transrational to
prerational, 88, 89–90
frontal personality system, 118–20
fulcrums, stages of development and,
68–69

Gardner, Howard, 56, 57
Gebser, Jean, 113
Gnostic conception of cause of illness, 168
God
immanence of, 1–2, 3–4
unity with, 18
Goodness, 104
Great Chain of Being, 49–54
completing the, 108–14
development of levels of, 115–22
failure to grasp evolution, 113–14
failure to recognize psychopathologies,
112–13
hierarchical nature of, 50–54
integral approach to, 102–4
levels of, 49, 118 (*see also* structures of
consciousness)

quadrants of, 108
subdivisions of mind within, 109–12
traditional depiction of, 111–12, 118
Great Holarchy of Being, 53. *See also* Great
Chain of Being
Great Mother, as archetype, 148–49
Great Nest of Being, 50. *See also* Great
Chain of Being
Great Search, 13, 14
gross level of being, at time of death,
170–71
gross-subtle-causal cycle in sleep, 156–59
Ground of Being
immutable union with, 95–98
involution and, 98–100

Habermas, Jürgen, rationality, 92–93
Hakuin, 2
hara, 77
Heart, as core, 29
Heisenberg, Werner, 16
heterarchy, relation to hierarchy, 58–59, 60
hierarchy
described, 50–51
holarchical nature of, 115–17
manifestation of Spirit as, 53
nonlinearity of, 55–60
Hinayana, 123–24
Hofstadter, Douglas, 62
holarchy
nature of hierarchy, 115–17
described, 53–54
dominator, 64
indefiniteness of, 64
holistic beliefs, spirituality and, 183
holistic conception of cause of illness, 169
holons
described, 50
hierarchy and, 55–60
reality composed of, 61–64
hostility, projection and suppression of,
78–79
humor, transcendence and, 185

I, we, it, 101
integral approach, 102–4
idiot compassion, 153
I-I, Self as, 27–30. *See also* Self; Witness
illness
contrasted with sickness, 162–69
cultural conceptions of causes of,
167–69

images, contrasted with symbols and concepts, 70
infantile state, Romantic view of, 95–98
inner witness. *See* Witness
insight meditation, 123–24
integral approach to reality, 102–4
integral practice, 105–7, 183
integral psychograph, as holarchy, 116–17
integral yoga, 105
integration of bodymind, 73–74
intellecual, experiential, and spiritual, 85–87
intuition of Oneness, faith and belief and, 178–79, 182
involution, 98
involutionary arc, 157
ishtadeva (divine forms), 71

Jakobson, Roman, 56, 57
Jeans, Sir James, mysticism and, 16, 18
jivanmukta (liberated one), 30
judgments, spiritual awareness and, 153–55
Julian, Dame, 2
Jung, Carl
    archetypes and mysticism, 147–49
    elevating prerational to transrational, 89
just this, 186

Kalu Rinpoche, 125
karma, relation to illness, 168
Keating, Father Thomas, 184
Keter, 67
Knower, absolute, 23–24
koans, practice of, 180–81
Koestler, Arthur, 50, 53, 60
koshas (sheaths), 53
Kosmos, composition of, 64

language, as boundary, 22–23
Lankavatara Sutra, 25
Lao Tzu, 23–24
Leonard, George, 105
Loevinger, Jane, 73
Lowen, Alexander, 75
lucid dreaming, 158

magical conception of cause of illness, 169
magic belief, 177
magic stage of development, 66, 70, 109
Maha-ati, 127, 131

Mahamudra, 127
Mahayana, 124–26
manas (subtle realm), 41, 66, 71
manomayakosha (mind level), 41, 66, 71
manovijñana (mind level), 41, 66, 71
matriarchal religions, view of Spirit, 52
matter. *See also* structures of consciousness
    integral approach to, 102–4
    level of Great Chain of Being, 49
maya (manifest world), 53
McDermott, Robert, 153–55
medical conception of cause of illness, 168
meditation
    aspects of, 5
    Dzogchen and, 132–33
    insight, 123–24
    nonduality and, 12–15
    purpose of, 17
    relation of integral practice to, 182–83
    as spiritual practice, 5–6
Mencken, H. L., 185
mental level of consciousness, 43
mind. *See also* psychic; psychological level of consciousness; structures of consciousness
    dream state and, 156–57
    integral approach to, 102–4
    level of Great Chain of Being, 49
    stages of growth, 109
    subdivisions of, 109–12
mu (koan), 180–81
Murphy, Michael, 105
muscles
    as agents of emotional suppression, 78–80
    releasing suppressed emotion from, 80–84
mysticism
    archetypes and, 147–49
    levels of, 181
    nonduality and, 12
    physicists and, 16–20
    relation of physics to, 18–20
mystics, message of, 3–4
mythic belief, 177
mythic stage of development, 66, 70–71, 109–10

narcissists, 33
nefesh (ego), 4
neti, neti, 27

neurosis, Freud's concept of, 88
New Age movement, 111
   conception of cause of illness, 168
new paradigm, 111
nirvikalpa samadhi, 29, 182
no-boundary awareness, 22, 26
nonduality. *See also* unity
   meditation and, 13–15
   obstacles to perception of, 12–13
   peak experiences, 179, 182
   realization of, 128–30
   Spirit and, 52
   ultimate nature of reality, 8
nondual stage of development, 110

observer, of the self, 10
one hand clapping, 128–30
One Taste, 13, 34–35
   constrasted with Witnessing, 159–61
   gross-subtle-causal cycle and, 158–59
   nature of, 129–30
   obstacles to, 135–38
   relation to spiritual practice, 138–39
Original Face (koan), 172–73

Patanjali, 39
pathologies, stages of development and, 68–69
patriarchal religions, view of Spirit, 52
Pauli, Wolfgang, mysticism and, 16, 18
peak experiences, of the transpersonal, 179–80, 182
pellucid dreaming, 158
perennial philosophy
   core of, 8, 108
   Great Chain of Being and, 49–54
   seven essentials of, 8
   as spiritual worldview, 7–8
permanent adaptation, stage of spiritual unfolding, 181–82
personality systems, 118–22
perspectivism, 92–94
phantasmic-emotional structure of consciousness, 70
physical level of consciousness, 41–43
   sensoriphysical, 70
physicists, mysticism and, 16–20
physics, mysticism and, 18–20
Planck, Max, mysticism and, 16
plateau experiences, of the transpersonal, 180–81, 182

pleasure, breathing exercise and, 76–77
Plotinus, polemics and, 154
pneuma, 4
pointing-out instructions, 132–34
polemics, value of, 153–55
Prabhavananda, Swami, 21
practice. *See* integral practice; spiritual practice
pranamayakosha (biological realm), 41, 65
prayer
   centering, 184
   petitionary, 6
prepersonal. *See* prerational
prerational, the
   contrasted with the transrational, 88–91
   realm of development, 67
pre/trans fallacy, 88–91. *See also* Romantic view
psychic, the. *See also* mind; psychological level of consciousness
   division of Vajrayana, 127
   peak experiences, 179–80, 182
   stage of development, 66, 71, 110
   structure of consciousness, 71
psychological conception of cause of illness, 168
psychological level of consciousness, 41–43
psychopathologies, failure of Great Chain of Being to recognize, 112–13

quadrants
   of Great Chain of Being, 108
   integral practice and, 105–7
   of levels of existence, 103
Quantum Questions (Wilber) 16, 18

Ramana Maharshi, Sri, 8, 24, 44, 133, 134, 172, 174
   on the I-I, 27–30
rational belief, 177
rationality, perspectivism and, 92–94
rational, the
   realm of development, 67
   stage of development, 66, 71, 110
reality
   composed of holons, 61–64
   integral approach to, 102–4
   multidimensional nature of, 49
   ultimate nature of, 8, 21–22
real self, contradictions of, 21–26. *See also* Self

reincarnation, 170–71
religion
    academic, 152
    matriarchal and patriarchal, 52
    translative and transformative, 140–43
representational mind (rep-mind), structure
    of consciousness, 70
Romantic view
    of infantile state, 95–98
    involution and, 98
ruach (divine spirit), 4
rule/role mind, structure of consciousness,
    71

sages, egolessness of, 31–32, 34
sahaja (constant consciousness), 181–82
sahaj samadhi, 13
samsara, 157
Sangha, 101
satori, 181
savikalpa samadhi, 182
Schrödinger, Erwin
    on eternal being, 173–74
    mysticism and, 16, 20
    on unity, 16–17, 18
Schwartz, Tony, 105
scientific conception of cause of illness, 169
Seer, absolute, 22, 23–25
sefirot (levels of awareness), 53
self. *See also* ego; Self; self-contraction
    disidentification from individual, 38–40
    observer of, 10
    separate, 17, 140–43
Self. *See also* real self; self; Witness
    before parents were born, 172–73,
        174–75
    dreamless sleep and, 157, 174–75
    as I-I, 27–30
    one hundred years from now, 173–75
    tonglen practice and, 126
self-contraction, obstacle to One Taste,
    135–37
sensorimotor stage of development, 109
sensoriphysical structure of consciousness,
    70
Shankara, 160
    on Reality, 21–22
Shibyama, Zen Master, 22
sleep, gross-subtle-causal cycle in, 156–59.
    See also dreamless sleep, dreams
Smith, Huston, 51, 118

soul. *See also* deeper psychic personality
        system; structures of consciousness
    contrasted with spirit, 4
    dream state and, 156–57
    integral approach to, 102–4
    level of Great Chain of Being, 49
    at time of death, 170–71
    transpersonal nature of, 9–11
spectrum of consciousness
    nine basic structures, pathologies, and
        treatments, 67–72
    seven stages and three realms, 65–67
spirit. *See also* Spirit; structures of
        consciousness
    contrasted with soul, 4
    integral approach to, 102–4
    level of Great Chain of Being, 49
Spirit. *See also* spirit
    as aspect of nonduality, 12–15, 52
    as ever-present awareness, 44–46
    futilely seeking, 98, 99
    hierarchical nature of, 53
    omnipresence of, 131–34
    transcendental and immanent nature of,
        51–52
    Vajrayana and, 126–27
spiritual, experiential, and intellectual,
    85–87
spiritual development, relation of integral
    practice to, 182–83
spiritual evolution, 98–99. *See also*
    spiritual unfolding
spirituality
    countercultural, 111, 112
    the prerational/transrational fallacy and,
        88–91
    relation of rationality and vision-logic to,
        92–94
spiritual practice. *See also* meditation
    koans, 180–81
    necessity of, 180–82, 183–84
    relation to One Taste, 138–39
    tonglen, 124–26
spiritual test, ultimate, 172–75
spiritual unfolding. *See also* spiritual evolu-
    tion
    four stages of, 176–82
    spiritual practice and, 182–84
stages of development. *See* development
structures of consciousness, nine basic, 68–
    72. *See also* consciousness

subtle, the
    dreaming and, 156–59
    level of consciousness, 41–43, 127
    peak experiences, 179, 182
    stage of development, 66–67, 71–72,
        110
    structure of consciousness, 71–72
    at time of death, 170–71
symbols, contrasted with images and
    concepts, 70
systems theory, hierarchy and, 55–60

tantras, divisions of Vajrayana, 127
Tao of Physics, (Capra), 18–19
tat tvam asi (Thou are That), 3
tension. *See* blocks
Teresa, Saint, 32
Tertullian, 89
Thomas, Saint, 39
Thou are That, 3
Tibetan Book of the Dead, 157
tonglen practice, 124–26
transfinite, meaning of, 62
transformation, function of religion,
    140–43
translation
    belief and, 177–78
    function of religion, 140–43
transpersonal, the. *See also* transrational
    direct experience of levels of, 179–81,
        182
    experience of, 10–11
    relation of rationality to, 92–94
    as term, 9–10
transrational, the. *See also* transpersonal
    contrasted with the prerational, 88–91
    realm of development, 67
treatment methods, stages of development
    and, 68–69
Trungpa, Chögyam, 51, 153
Truth, 104
turiya (ultimate reality), 72
turiyatita (fifth state), 159
"turtles all the way down" (joke), 61

ultimate level of consciousness, 41–43
unity, consciousness of, 16–17, 18. *See also*
    nonduality; unity consciousness
unity consciousness, 13
    contrasted with Witness, 37–38
    difficulty in describing, 22–23
upward causation, 58

Vajrayana, 126–127
    divisions of, 127
vasanas, 67
vijñanamayakosha (subtle realm), 41, 66,
    72
vijñanas (levels of awareness), 41, 53
vipassana (insight meditation), 123–24
vision-logic, 71
    relation to spirituality, 93–94
    stage of development, 110
vision-logic belief, 177
vital force, breathing exercise and, 77

Watts, Alan, 7
web-of-life ideologies, 111
Wei Wu Wei, 124
What Really Matters (Schwartz), 105
whole-minded, 46–47
wholism, limitations of concept, 61–64
Wilber, Treya Killam, 167, 169
wilber-3, 115–20
wilber levels (1–4), 115
Witness, 22, 23. *See also* observer; Self;
        Witness Exercise; Witnessing
    contrasted with unity consciousness,
        37–38
    dreamless sleep and, 156–60, 174
    dualistic nature of, 159
    as eternal being, 173–74
    experience and, 86–87
    as I-I, 27–30
    as Original Face, 172–73
    perceived as object, 135–37, 139
    personality system development and,
        120–21
    Self as, 27–28
Witness Exercise, 36–40
Witnessing
    contrasted with One Taste, 159–60
    disidentification and, 38–40
Wolf, Fred Alan, 19

yidam (divine forms), 71

Zenrin, 172
Zukav, Gary, 19